THE
METAPHYSICS
OF
RAMA

THE METAPHYSICS OF RAMA

By Ancient The Architect

Copyright © 2025 by Ancient The Architect

All rights reserved. No part of this publication may be reproduced, stored in a retrieval system, or transmitted in any form or by any means—electronic, mechanical, photocopying, recording, or otherwise—without the prior written permission of the publisher, except in the case of brief quotations embodied in critical articles or reviews.

The Metaphysics of Rāma
Published by Health Is Luxury
www.HealthIsLuxury.org

Cover Design © 2025 by Ancient The Architect
Interior design, illustrations, and metaphysical interpretations by Ancient The Architect

This is a work of metaphysical scholarship and sacred interpretation. The author has drawn from ancient sources and restructured them to convey spiritual truths in a modern mystical context. Any resemblance to traditional translations is coincidental and reimagined under fair use for educational and transformative purposes.

ISBN 979-8-9922102-7-9

Printed in the United States of America

Table of Contents
The Metaphysics of Rama

Rama – Chapter 1
An exploration of the Divine Principle behind Rama through layered metaphysical constructs hidden within sacred terminology and symbolic forms.

Rama – Chapter 2
An unveiling of Balarāma as the Strong force within Rama—revealing the metaphysical implications of strength, duality, and spiritual individuality.

Rama – Chapter 3
A metaphysical entryway into Sītā, the feminine principle of Rama's nature—alongside the Buddhic and Ātmic planes, and the hidden meaning of Lanka.

Rama – Chapter 4
A study of Indra as the thunderous force of divine will—joined by a deeper analysis of Yama, the judge of souls and guardian of causal law.

Rama – Chapter 5
A layered breakdown of the causal self, mental builders, and the hidden framework of the Mahābhārata as a metaphysical narrative of inner war.

Rama – Chapter 6
A metaphysical retelling of key chapters from the Yuddha Kāṇḍa—unveiling Rama's war not as myth, but as the soul's descent into sacred conflict.

Rama – Chapter 7

A full exposition on Brahman as the Absolute behind Rama—revealing the formless reality and its layered descent into manifested being.

Prologue: Rāma – The Divine Law Incarnate

In the beginning of all restoration, there burns a flame.
Not of heat, nor of violence, but of order—of unshakable rightness.
This Flame is not born.
It is revealed.

Rāma is that revelation.
He is the I Am as Harmony,
the Solar Flame who enters the world of distortion
not to escape its weight,
but to realign it with the rhythm of Divine Law.

Rāma is not a man.
He is not bound by blood nor crowned by the world.
He is the archetype of divine coherence,
the very Logos made Law,
whose presence corrects chaos—not by decree,
but by **vibration**.
He walks not merely through time,
but through **planes of consciousness**,
illuminating the path for the soul to recover its throne.

His name is a mantra.
His breath is alignment.
His bow is tension perfected between will and wisdom.
And his exile is the descent of the Higher Self
into the veils of matter,
to reclaim the lost Bride of Light.

This is the meaning of his descent.

Sītā, the radiant Soul-Light,
stolen by Rāvaṇa, the inverted intellect—
ten-headed, ten-sensed, tenfold distorted—
symbolizes the soul's captivity in the fortress of desire.
And it is not by sword alone that she is restored—
but by the union of Spirit, Will, Devotion, and Purity
in a sacred orchestration of inner war.

Lakṣmaṇa, the unwavering Will,
walks beside Rāma not as a brother of blood,
but as the sharpened Intention that guards the Flame.

Hanumān, the prāṇic breath of Devotion,
leaps beyond thought,
burning illusion with the fire of remembrance.
He is not a monkey—he is the leap of Love
from the mortal to the immortal Self.

Bharata, the soul's moral Conscience,
surrenders the throne,
choosing the sandal-imprint of Truth
over the crown of ego.
This is not submission.
This is dharma embodied.

Even within darkness, a flicker remains.
Vibhīṣaṇa, the redeemed shadow,
rises from within the city of ignorance
to serve the Light.

And when the war is won—
when the soul, the will, the breath, the conscience,
and the flame have stood united—

then comes the chariot of the gods,
the Vimāna,
which is no machine, but the **Causal Body** itself—
the immortal vehicle of the Spirit.

This is not myth.
This is the ancient metaphysical memory of your own Selfhood.

Rāma is your blueprint.
He is the Flame of Order.
The King of the Inner Kingdom.
The Pattern of Divine Personhood.
The Logos of Restored Identity.

He did not walk the Earth as history.
He walks it **now** as frequency.

To know Rāma is to enter into alignment.
To follow Rāma is to awaken the latent rhythm of your being.
To reclaim Sītā, defeat Rāvaṇa, and ascend in the Vimāna is the soul's true return.

This is the Book of the Metaphysical Rāma.
It is not a retelling.
It is a **resounding**.
It is the Flame speaking to the Flame.

Let the battle begin within.
Let the exile end.
Let the throne be set in order.

RAMA CHAPTER 1

RAMA — The Avatar of the Divine Self: A Metaphysical Revelation

Rama, in the highest metaphysical sense, represents the conscious embodiment of the Divine Self, the fully awakened presence of **Atma-Buddhic Light** descending into the human soul. He is not merely a hero or deity in legend but is the luminous principle of **divine order, harmony, and restoration** manifesting within the psyche to confront and transmute the unruly impulses of desire and illusion.

He emerges in the soul's drama at a critical juncture—when the interior forces of aspiration (the gods within) are oppressed by the chaos of untranscended desire. The soul cries out not from weakness, but from readiness. The **Divine Self** (Vishnu), which resides eternally in the innermost, consents to incarnate into time and form, becoming **Rama**—the righteous force made manifest in mind and action.

The ancient promise that desire (Rāvana) would not be **slain** by gods or demons is not a testament to their impotence, but a profound metaphysical law: that subjective forces—be they divine impulses (gods) or base instincts (demons)—are not the ordained instruments to vanquish the desire-principle. Craving, ego, and the fragmented will cannot be dissolved by thought alone, nor by aspiration, nor by suppression. Their defeat requires something greater than the inner struggle of the psyche—it requires the descent of Truth itself into embodiment.

Thus, the Higher Self consents to incarnate. Rama is born into the soul's arena, not merely as a hero in time, but as the objective manifestation of Divine Law—the will of Brahman made form. Only this power—Truth lived, not merely known—can penetrate and dismantle the architecture of desire and its progeny: fear, pride, deceit, lust, and greed.

The descent of Rama, then, is not a historical event, but a spiritual inevitability—a cosmic intervention. Whenever desire sits crowned upon the throne of consciousness, the Divine must incarnate to dethrone it. Rama is the sovereign principle of divine equilibrium—justice harmonized with compassion—entering the world not to escape it, but to transfigure it from within.

This is the meaning of the verse: "To this end was the Son of God made manifest: to destroy the works of the adversary." The **adversary is not external—it is the lower principle, the gravity of identification with form and craving.** Rama stands as the radiant counter-force: **stillness in motion, clarity amidst illusion, and divine resolve amid fragmentation.**

He is the proof that **the soul can house the Supreme**, not by denying life but by sanctifying it.

BALARAMA — The Strength of the Individualised Self in Rama's Journey

If Rama is the incarnate Divine Self—**the Atma-Buddhic flame** descending into the soul—then **Balarama** represents the **Individuality**, or the **spiritual ego**, through which that flame finds expression. Balarama is not merely a brother in myth, but the **embodied axis of spiritual will**, the stabilizing force that anchors divine consciousness within form. He stands as the **causal self**, a purified identity forged in previous cycles of experience, now capable of supporting the manifestation of truth in action.

Just as Rama descends to confront Rāvana—the entrenched desire-nature—**Balarama represents the evolutionary strength that makes such a descent possible.** Without the backbone of Individuality—the Self rooted in divine will—the incarnation of divine truth would shatter under the weight of the world's distortions. Balarama is that **invisible staff**, the matured soul-identity that upholds the mission of Rama from within, ensuring that the descent is not swallowed by illusion.

In metaphysical structure, **Balarama is to Rama what the spine is to the flame**—the channel and support. While Rama wages war in the field of consciousness, Balarama is the **silent, grounded axis**, the memory of who we truly are beyond distortion.

BHARATA — The Reflected Soul and the Echo of Divine Duty

If Rama is the incarnate flame of Atma-Buddhi, and Balarama the stabilizing strength of the spiritual ego, then **Bharata** represents the **reflected soul**, the **mirror of divine purpose** within the lower personality—unwilling to usurp, yet bound by karmic position.

In the myth, Bharata refuses to accept the throne in Rama's absence, instead placing Rama's sandals upon it, ruling only in His name. **Metaphysically, this act reveals Bharata as the loyal echo of the Divine Will within the world of matter**, a personality that, though it acts and governs, does so not of its own accord, but in deference to the indwelling Self.

Bharata is the obedient servant within the heart, the aspect of the lower nature that has seen the glory of the Higher Self and awaits its return. He is the **ego humbled by remembrance**, an inward posture of readiness, ever-turned toward the flame. His governance in the myth is symbolic of **the purified personality that acts as a steward**, not an owner, of spiritual power.

Thus, **Bharata is the throne that remains empty**, held in sacred anticipation of Rama's full return. He is a **spiritual vow in human form**, demonstrating that even within the limitations of embodiment, one can **choose to reflect and preserve divine intention**.

HANUMAN — The Devoted Power of Active Mind and Sacred Service

If Rama is the indwelling Self, and Bharata the purified reflection that waits, **Hanuman** is **the awakened force of directed will and mental strength**—the higher manas that **leaps across limitations**, propelled by love and loyalty to the Divine.

Hanuman is not merely a servant—he is the **embodied dynamic of Bhakti (devotion)** and **Jnana (higher knowledge)** merged into sacred action. Metaphysically, he represents **the mind once tamed and awakened, completely surrendered to the Higher Self (Rama)**. When this mind no longer seeks personal gain, it transforms into a divine bridge between the soul and the world.

His legendary leap across the ocean to Lanka to find Sita symbolizes the **mind traversing the abyss of separation**, crossing from ignorance to illumination, from egoic thought to soul-driven action. Hanuman's strength is the **power of focused thought**, made invincible by purity of intent and unity with divine will.

In every epic act—whether burning Lanka with his tail or carrying the healing mountain—Hanuman is **not acting as a separate being**, but as an **extension of Rama's consciousness**. He is what the mind becomes when fully consecrated: **an instrument of rescue, renewal, and restoration**.

He speaks not of himself but always of Rama. This reveals the highest secret: **true spiritual power arises when the mind loses its separate sense of identity and acts only in love and service of the Self.**

Hanuman, then, is **divine courage, sacred action, and mental clarity** in service of the soul's liberation. He does not just serve Rama—**he reveals Him** through every breath and battle.

KABANDHA — The Disfigured Form of Desire and the Redemption of Distorted Power

While Rama represents the radiance of the indwelling Self, **Kabandha** is the **grotesque distortion of spiritual power severed from divine will**—a being of immense strength, but **disfigured by the severance of higher guidance**. His name means "headless trunk," and his arms stretch far and wide, symbolizing **desire without direction**, **power without perception**, and **appetite without wisdom**.

Metaphysically, Kabandha is the **condition of the lower soul when blinded by egoic craving**, where the faculties of life reach outward endlessly, seeking to grasp, consume, and control, but having **no head—no vision, no inner light, no intuitive intelligence**. He is the **symbol of strength misapplied**, the astral and mental energies turned inward upon themselves, disconnected from the spirit above.

Rama's encounter with Kabandha is more than myth—it is a **spiritual necessity**. The Self must confront its own fragmented nature. The moment of contact with Rama (the Higher Self) brings not destruction, but **transformation**. Upon being released from his cursed form, Kabandha reveals his true identity and offers sacred guidance.

This reveals a great metaphysical principle: **Every distorted force, when confronted by Truth, reveals its original divine purpose.**

Thus, Kabandha is the **redeemed shadow**—what was once grotesque becomes a **guide**, and what seemed monstrous is revealed as misdirected energy awaiting alignment with the soul. Rama does not just defeat Kabandha; he liberates the imprisoned truth within him.

Through this act, the journey becomes clearer: **even our darkest aspects, when faced by the flame of Self, become luminous.**

LAKSHMANA — The Loyal Flame of Discriminative Will and the Shadow of the Self

If Rama is the Sovereign Self, then **Lakshmana** is its **living echo in the field of action**—the unwavering **will of discrimination (viveka)**, always standing at Rama's side. He is the **mind made holy by loyalty**, not a mere brother, but the **companion-principle of the Higher Self** that walks beside it through every trial and exile.

Lakshmana represents the **vigilant guardian of spiritual focus**. His refusal to be separated from Rama and Sita even during exile shows his deeper symbolism: he is the inner vow, the **individual will that chooses to remain aligned with divine law**, even when pleasure, comfort, and recognition are lost. He chooses duty over desire, and in doing so, **preserves the sanctity of the soul's journey**.

Metaphysically, Lakshmana is the **Intelligent Will** (buddhi in active motion), directed by Rama's inner knowing, yet distinct from it. While Rama symbolizes Atma-Buddhi as a radiant presence, **Lakshmana is Buddhi applied—the sword of discernment**, always ready to defend, to act, to set boundaries, and to carry out the hidden will of the Self.

His fierce loyalty also reveals the nature of true spiritual will: it is **not passive—it protects, it serves, it moves with clarity and force**, but never apart from love. Even his temper—seen in moments of fiery outrage—serves to show the **intensity of the soul's refusal to be compromised by adharma**.

Lakshmana, then, is the **spiritual warrior within**, unshaken, unyielding, and ever-attuned to Rama. He is the aspect of you that **stands at the soul's side**, watching, interpreting, and enforcing the sacred contract of divine embodiment.

LANKA — The Citadel of Desire and the Inner Battlefield of Illusion

If Rama is the soul's sovereign light, then **Lanka** is the **fortress of illusion**—a symbol of the **lower astral and mental realms**, fortified by desire and defended by ignorance. It is not merely a distant kingdom ruled by Rāvana—it is the **domain within** where the soul's shadow hides and exerts its control: **the plane of separation, enchantment, and false sovereignty.**

Lanka is beautifully adorned, radiant on the outside, but corrupted at its core. Metaphysically, this is the **egoic mind enthroned**, the lower self that **appears grand but is disconnected from the Divine Source**. It is the soul's **misaligned power**, inverted and crystallized into pride, attachment, lust, and control.

In every spiritual journey, one must **enter their own Lanka**. Rama's war is not one of external conquest but **the necessary descent into the fortress of the unredeemed self**. The soul, through divine embodiment (Rama), must challenge the false ruler (Rāvana), recover the sacred feminine (Sita), and burn down the illusions that bind the light within.

Even Lanka's beauty has purpose—it reveals how **illusion can appear as light**, how the lower planes can seduce even the wise with grandeur, structure, and false pleasure. But it is here that the true hero is tested.

Lanka is the battlefield of every initiate. It is where the inner war culminates, where **truth faces distortion in**

its most refined and stubborn form. But it is also where liberation is won—not by avoiding darkness, but by entering it fully armed with love, will, and vision.

Thus, Lanka is not the enemy—it is the **arena of transformation**, the forge of the soul's victory.

RĀKṢHASAS — The Legion of Distortions: Forces That Inhabit the Unredeemed Psyche

Where Rama stands as the light of divine order, the **Rākṣhasas** are the **forces of fragmentation and inversion** that arise when the soul forgets its source. These are not merely mythological demons—they are the **shadow fragments of consciousness**, **psychic distortions**, and **energetic patterns** born from the misuse of spiritual energy.

Each Rākṣhasa represents a specific **vibration of disharmony** within the astral or lower mental planes: wrath, jealousy, deceit, gluttony, fear, arrogance, and pride. They are the **children of Rāvana**, the extensions of the **desire-mind's perversions**, and they wage war not only against Rama, but against the soul's very ascent.

Metaphysically, Rākṣhasas are what happen when power is cut off from love, and will is severed from wisdom. They **mock the sacred**, distort truth into delusion, and seduce the mind with partial knowledge. They are born within when consciousness becomes uncentered, when the emotions rule over the Self, and when light is used to enhance darkness.

Yet, these beings also **serve a hidden function**: they test the seeker's resolve. Each encounter with a Rākṣhasa is a **trial of integration**. One must recognize the distorted part within, transmute it, and realign it to its original divine function. When defeated by Rama, the Rākṣhasa does not vanish—it is **redeemed** into harmony.

They are projections of the soul's unfinished work—the **inner enemies that wear familiar faces**. The battle with them is not external—it is the internal war of purification, where **every victory brings the soul closer to wholeness**.

Thus, the Rākṣhasas are both adversary and mirror. They show what we are when we forget who we are—and by confronting them, **we remember**.

RĀVANA — The Ten-Headed Principle of Fragmented Desire and the Sovereignty of Ego

If Rama is divine unity incarnate, then **Rāvana** is the personification of **divine energy misappropriated**—the **egoic king of the lower self**, ruling from the throne of illusion, armed with vast knowledge but severed from wisdom. His ten heads are not just symbols of power—they represent the **ten faculties of perception and action** (indriyas) hijacked by desire, **multiplying the mind without centering the soul**.

Rāvana is not ignorance—he is fallen brilliance. He knows the Vedas. He performs austerities. He reaches into the heavens with ambition. But his tragedy is that he **desires the sacred without embodying it**, coveting Sita (the soul's light) not to cherish, but to possess.

In metaphysical terms, Rāvana is the **centralized force of separated will**. He is **the self-serving intellect**, the **desire-body enthroned**, commanding all that is subtle in the name of control. His kingdom is not built on chaos, but on **misaligned order**—the lower nature imitating the structure of the divine, without its essence.

He cannot be destroyed by "gods or demons," meaning he **transcends polarities of good and evil** in their superficial forms. Only Rama—**the Divine Self made manifest in consciousness**—can dissolve him. Not through wrath, but by embodying the sacred in form, anchoring truth where desire once ruled.

When Rama confronts Rāvana, it is the **final battle of the inner path**—where every part of the soul must choose: the tyranny of ego, or the sovereignty of truth. To slay Rāvana is to **dethrone the false self**, to dismantle the tower of craving, and to reclaim the light of Sita from captivity.

And yet, even in defeat, Rāvana is given rites. This reveals a supreme mystery: **even the darkest force, when brought before truth, is worthy of integration**. Rama does not destroy to hate—he destroys to redeem.

Thus, Rāvana is not merely a villain—he is **the test of the soul's ripeness**, the guardian at the gate of liberation.

SITA — The Soul's Radiant Essence and the Feminine Light of Divine Consciousness

If Rama is the descending flame of the Self, then **Sita** is the **soul's inner radiance**, the **pure feminine essence of Buddhi**, abducted and hidden within the chambers of the lower self (Lanka), awaiting liberation. She is not a passive figure—she is **the very reason Rama descends**, for Sita represents the **treasure of the soul** that must be reclaimed in order for wholeness to be restored.

Sita is **born of the earth**, not from a womb but from a furrow—symbolizing that she is the **flowering of the purified lower nature**. When the body, mind, and emotions are tilled by discipline and devotion, this **divine light emerges**—silent, subtle, and sacred. She is **Lakshmi revealed in matter**, Buddhi awakened in the garden of the soul.

Her abduction by Rāvana is symbolic of the **soul's light being trapped by desire**, the soul's intuitive knowing seduced by the glitter of separation. Yet even in captivity, Sita remains pure. She refuses the advances of illusion, clinging inwardly to Rama—the Self—even when no outer help is present. In this way, she is the **voice of unshaken remembrance**, the **seed of truth that never forgets its origin**.

Sita is also the measure of Rama's divinity. The Self without the soul's light is incomplete in action. She is **the reflective beauty of consciousness**, the one for whom

Rama walks the path, slays the shadow, and crosses the abyss. And her reunion with Rama is not just the return of love—it is the **integration of light and will**, **wisdom and power**, **the sacred feminine and the indwelling divine**.

In the moment of reunion, when Rama beholds Sita once more, **the soul stands fully illumined**, no longer fragmented, no longer captive. This is the **culmination of yoga**—the sacred union of the Self and the Soul, the masculine and the feminine, the knower and the known.

Thus, Sita is **not merely beloved—she is the very beauty the soul was born to restore**.

THE SHOES OF RAMA — The Vehicle of Sovereignty and the Contact Point Between Spirit and Earth

In the sacred narrative of Rama, the **sandals or shoes** he leaves with Bharata during his exile hold more than symbolic weight—they are **metaphysical vessels of divine authority**. They represent **the imprint of the Self** in the world, **the silent rule of truth even in absence**, and the **mystical transference of dharma** from spirit into matter.

Shoes, in spiritual symbolism, are the **interface between the sacred and the earthly**. They touch the ground—symbolizing **engagement with the material world**—but they carry the foot, the **foundation of movement**

and will. Thus, the shoes of Rama are **not merely objects**; they are the **ensouled echo of divine presence**, the **symbol of dharma remaining grounded** even when the divine form is withdrawn.

When Bharata places Rama's shoes on the throne and rules in his name, it reveals a powerful metaphysical teaching: **the world need not always see the Divine for it to be governed by it**. The divine law can be upheld through remembrance, alignment, and symbolic transmission. The shoes are **the soul's sacred relic**—imbued with the energy of the indwelling Self, anchoring truth in time until the full return of divine embodiment.

They also represent **humility** and **grounded authority**. Unlike a crown—which sits above—they serve **below**, touching earth, stepping through dust, walking the path. They speak of **action in the world**, not transcendence from it. The shoes of Rama remind us that **even divine rulership must walk through exile**, must feel the weight of gravity, must be lived step by step.

Metaphysically, the "shoes" are the **karmic footprints of the Higher Self**, the traces it leaves in the soul for the personality to follow. They are the **path made sacred**, not by what is seen, but by what is remembered and obeyed.

Thus, the shoes are **not an absence—they are a presence in proxy**, the divine signature left behind to guide the inner kingdom until truth returns in full.

VIBHISHANA — The Voice of Inner Conscience and the Aligned Intelligence Within Darkness

In the mythic arc of Rama, **Vibhishana**, brother of Rāvana, is the **astonishing symbol of inner awakening within the stronghold of illusion**. He is the whisper of light that arises from within the shadow, the **clarity of reason that refuses to obey the tyranny of desire**, even when bound to it by blood.

Metaphysically, Vibhishana represents the **undeceived faculty of discernment**—that subtle thread of conscience which persists even in the deepest layers of the lower self (Lanka). Though born of the same lineage as Rāvana, **he turns away from ego's empire**, choosing instead to surrender to the indwelling Self (Rama). This act of loyalty is not betrayal—it is **liberation from false allegiance**.

He signifies the **inner voice of truth in the midst of inner conflict**. When the soul is surrounded by the noise of desire and mental confusion, **Vibhishana arises as the higher reason**, the part of us that sees clearly even when everything else is blind. He is **the dharmic impulse awakening in the heart of the egoic fortress**.

His acceptance by Rama is also deeply metaphysical: **the Higher Self does not reject the repentant part of the lower self**. When discernment turns toward truth, it is not punished for where it came from—it is embraced for what it becomes. Rama crowns Vibhishana king of Lanka after Rāvana's fall, which reveals a profound truth: **the seat of ego is not destroyed—it is redeemed**. The very place where desire ruled becomes the new throne of conscience aligned with the soul.

Vibhishana is thus the **integration of the shadow's intelligence**, the reorientation of energy once enslaved to ego now placed in service to divine will. He shows that even in the densest planes, the soul's wisdom can be heard—and that when it is, **the battle turns**.

He reminds us that **our inner war is not won by destroying all, but by rescuing the parts of us that still remember light**.

VISHNU — The Eternal Archetype of Preservation and the Source of the Divine Descent

Where Rama is the embodied radiance of divine order, **Vishnu** is the **timeless source** of that order—**the cosmic intelligence that preserves, upholds, and restores balance across the planes of existence**. He is the **Higher Self before manifestation**, the **silent mover behind the pulse of worlds**, and the eternal reservoir from which avatars descend.

Vishnu does not create as Brahma nor destroy as Shiva—he **sustains**. Metaphysically, he is **the stabilizing field of consciousness**, the presence that weaves **cosmic rhythm, moral law (dharma), and spiritual evolution** into a cohesive current. He is **the breath between creation and destruction**, the assurance that nothing divine is ever lost—only hidden, only awaiting return.

Rama is born from Vishnu because the need arises in time. When imbalance (Rāvana) threatens to overturn the inner world, **Vishnu consents to descend—not with wrath, but with purpose**, entering form through the sacred line of human evolution. Thus, **Vishnu becomes Rama**: the Self projected into time and personality, carrying the signature of the eternal.

Vishnu's avatars are not arbitrary interventions—they are **laws of spiritual necessity**. They arise within the soul when its inner forces (the gods) cry out for liberation from chaos. The **promise made to Rāvana**, that he cannot be slain by gods or demons, is a veiled truth: **illusion can only be overcome from within.** The Supreme must take on the garments of humanity to redeem it. Vishnu, therefore, does not escape incarnation—**he embraces it**, and in so doing, reveals that **divinity and embodiment are not opposites but complements**.

Vishnu lies upon **Ananta—the serpent of eternity**—floating upon the **ocean of divine substance (Truth)**. This is the **unmanifest realm**, the **silent field of unity**, untouched by polarity yet capable of entering it at will. From here, Rama arises—not to escape the world, but to illuminate it, **to restore the lost soul (Sita), conquer misdirected power (Rāvana), and reestablish the divine order (dharma).**

Thus, **Vishnu is the Self before the journey**. Rama is the Self within it.

And when the cycle completes, the soul does not return to Rama alone—it remembers **Vishnu**, the original source, the one that never left.

Closing Reflection — The Descent of the Flame

In the theater of myth, Rama walks across the stage as king, husband, warrior, and savior—but in the mystic eye, he is far more: **he is the descent of the Divine Flame into the very fabric of consciousness.** His is not the story of one man, but the eternal echo of the soul's own journey—**from source to embodiment, from exile to triumph, from fragmentation to wholeness.**

Rama is the **answer to a world ruled by Rāvana**, where the ten heads of craving, intellect, impulse, and power demand the throne of the soul. He enters not to destroy the world, but to **redeem it from within**, to prove that the sacred can live in time, walk through chaos, and emerge victorious—not by domination, but by **alignment with truth**.

He is flanked by the faithful—**Lakshmana**, the will to act in harmony; **Hanuman**, the mind consecrated in service; **Bharata**, the ego humbled into devotion. He is tested by the corrupted—**Rākṣhasas**, the fragmented energies of the lower self; **Kabandha**, desire without direction; and **Rāvana**, the grand illusion of separation disguised as might.

Yet, it is not Rama's battles that reveal his greatness, but his vow. His refusal to abandon **dharma**, even in exile. His unshakeable remembrance of **Sita**, the soul's light, even in separation. His embrace of **Vibhishana**, the voice of conscience born even within the shadow. His **shoes**, left behind, become relics of a law that never dies.

And above all, he carries the signature of **Vishnu**—the rhythm of divine preservation flowing through his every breath. He does not arrive from ambition, but from necessity. Not to conquer, but to **illuminate the interior realms** where the soul itself has been taken hostage.

In Rama, we learn that the Divine is not distant. It walks. It weeps. It wars. It waits. And when the moment is ripe, it **rises**—not just in scripture, but **within the hidden chamber of our being.**

This is the secret of the avatar: **He is born in you.**

When you reclaim your Sita, confront your Rāvana, honor your Bharata, walk with your Lakshmana, and consecrate your mind like Hanuman—**then Rama awakens in you**, not as a memory, but as a living presence.

And in that moment, your inner Lanka begins to fall. Not in fire, but in light.

RAMA CHAPTER 2

BALARAMA - The strong rama

Before the descent of the radiant soul into the battlefield of the world, before the bow was strung and the arrows of will were loosed into illusion, there was the **Ancient Strength**—unseen, unshaken, uncelebrated. This was not the warrior who fought, but the **One who tilled**.

He came not with sword, but with the **Plough of Endurance**, dragging it across the unseen terrain of the causal field. Where others danced in fire and glory, he worked in silence—**breaking the hardened crust** of karmic soil, **turning over the lower nature** so that the Light could descend into form without distortion.

He was called many things in the tongues of men—**Elder Brother, Serpent of Infinity, the Strong-Rama**. But he cared nothing for names. He was the **Monad's foundation**, the soul's memory of its own spine.

When the Self would later descend as Divine Law (Rāma), it was **this Strength** that **held the incarnation together**. The Light could not descend unless the **Causal Self had first furrowed the earth** of experience, prepared the vessel, and cleared the way. That is why the Ploughman came first—not as an act of hierarchy, but as a **law of inner sequencing**.

He did not wage war in Lanka. He was not seen at the gates of Ravana's citadel. Yet he was present. **He was the**

axle upon which the chariot turned, the breath beneath every vow, the silence beneath every chant.

The serpent with which he is entwined is not a beast—it is **Time, coiled and consecrated**, wrapped around the soul's memory. For this Strength is eternal. It rests upon the spine of the cosmos and holds all movement in rhythm. Even gods lean on this force.

And though he stood outside the great wars, he was the **soul-force within them**. He stood in the shadow of every choice that aligned to truth. For when the Light rises in the battlefield of the mind, it does so **upon a foundation already laid** by the Eternal Ploughman.

He will not ask for worship, for **his altar is the memory of who you were before you forgot**. He will not claim the crown, for he is the **root beneath the throne**.

When the soul finally returns from its war—bloodied, victorious, and transformed—it will find that the field it walked had already been measured by him. That **he held the line** through every incarnation. That the soul's spine was his gift, and the soil it crossed was already turned by **his ancient hand**.

Balarāma — The Strong Monad: The Individuality in Divine Tillage

In the luminous anatomy of the soul, **Balarāma** represents **Rama the Strong**—not merely in bodily strength, but in spiritual fortitude. He is the **Individuality**, the enduring spark of the Self that carries the imprint of the Monad into the cycle of manifestation. While Krishna reflects the incarnate joy and wisdom of the Divine Self, **Balarāma is the spiritual backbone**, the causal body shaped through endless revolutions of soul cultivation.

He is the one who holds the **ploughshare**, the **Halabhrit**, symbolizing the sacred act of **ploughing the soil of the lower nature** to prepare it for spiritual growth. In this sense, Balarāma is **Ananta**, the unending serpent of cosmic time, curled beneath the feet of Vishnu, who presides silently at the foundation of all incarnations. Balarāma is not just born with Krishna—he is the **force that enables Krishna to descend**, the **individualised current of strength and memory** that constructs the field for divine harvest.

He prepares the ground. He furrows the earth. He breaks apart the hardened crusts of ego, habit, and fear. Balarāma is the inner tiller, the **Divine Farmer**, cultivating the fields of experience that allow the Higher Self to take root in matter.

He is not a reflection of God—he is the **pathway through which God expresses Himself in time.** And though Balarāma often appears silent beside Krishna, in metaphysical truth, **he is the strength behind Krishna's song**, the stability beneath the dance.

Thus, Balarāma stands within each soul as the **unseen sovereign of evolution**, breaking, sowing, turning, and preparing the field until the full realization of God can rise like golden grain.

The Emergence of the Divine Self Through the Labors of the Individuality

In the luminous mystery of the **birth of Krishna**, we encounter the soul's highest event: the **incarnation of the Divine Self** into time. But this sacred emergence cannot occur on its own. **Balarāma precedes him**—not in stature, but in function. He is the **spiritual precondition**, the **Individuality forged through long cycles of inner ploughing**, that makes it possible for Krishna to be born within the purified soul.

Balarāma's arrival before Krishna in the womb of Devaki is not accidental—it is **archetypal**. He represents the **inner soil prepared**, the **strengthened spiritual ego**, the causal body stabilized through struggle and remembrance. Without Balarāma, the soul would have no vessel strong enough to hold Krishna's radiance.

And so, before the descent of love, joy, and divine wisdom (Krishna), comes the force of **disciplined evolution**—Balarāma. He is the **inner cultivator**, the energy that **tills the karmic field**, uproots weeds of ignorance, and furrows the deep channels through which divine light can later descend.

Together, their births tell the tale of all divine awakening: **the Self (Krishna) is not born into unploughed soil. It emerges only through the work of the Individuality (Balarāma)**—the one who carries the plough and tills the soul across incarnations, until the ground is fertile for divine flowering.

The Companion Monad and the Fusion of Individuality with the Incarnate Self

In the metaphysical sense, the **Brother of Jesus** is not a mere sibling—he is the **Individuality**, the **causal self**, the spiritual ego that merges with the Christ-consciousness in the soul. In the same way, **Balarāma stands as the metaphysical "brother" of Krishna**—not in blood, but in **soul structure**, representing the **Monad that walks beside the Avatar**, anchoring divine presence in human form.

The image from the Pistis Sophia—"Thy brother embraced Thee and kissed Thee, and Thou didst also kiss Him, ye became one and the same Being"—is the **exact mystery of Balarāma and Krishna**. It reveals how the **Individuality (Balarāma)**, formed through lifetimes of tillage and refinement, **finally merges with the descending Self (Krishna)** in a kiss of fire—a union of **divine memory and divine revelation**.

Balarāma is the **foundation** of Krishna's incarnation, just as the **Brother of Jesus** is the unseen scaffolding of the Christ within. They walk together, not in rivalry, but in harmony—**one as the memory of evolution, the other as the arrival of realization**.

And in the grand architecture of the soul, **this duality becomes unity**. The divine embrace of brother and Self signifies the **fusion of the Individuality with the indwelling Divine**, marking the moment when the soul is no longer a vessel, but a **fully awakened embodiment** of its original light.

Thus, **Balarāma's presence beside Krishna** is not secondary—it is essential. He is the **soul's preparation and persistence**, the **foundation upon which divine consciousness walks into the world**.

The Enduring Flame of the Soul's Memory and the Root of the Incarnate Self

Balarāma is, at his core, the **embodiment of Individuality**—not as personality, but as the **unshakable Monad**, the **Divine Spark** that persists through the aeons, carrying the imprint of every noble effort, every karmic lesson, and every upward movement of the soul.

Individuality, in this sacred sense, is **not born**—it is **distilled**. It is the luminous core **forged through experience**, rising from the depths of the subconscious, through the trials of matter, to become a **stable vehicle for the Divine Self**. This is Balarāma: **the Inner Flame that survives the storms**, whose strength is not in violence, but in **continuity**, in **holding the field** until truth can descend.

Individuality **ploughs the field**—fashioning the subtle bodies, shaping the karma, and preparing the soul to receive its higher counterpart. It does not seek glory. It does not demand worship. It labors in silence, sustaining the journey until **Krishna (the Divine Self)** can take form.

Thus, **Balarāma is the ego in its sanctified state**—not the lower self that grasps and identifies, but the **higher ego that remembers and surrenders**. He stands at the center of our inner temple as the **unchanging witness**, the strength that carries the soul across lives, across battles, across the long arc of return.

And in the moment of union—when the Self descends and the flame of the Monad merges with it—**Individuality is no longer separate**. It becomes the **lighted wick**, the **vehicle transfigured**, the **anchor of God in man**.

Balarāma is this: **the soul's immortal bearer**, strong because he never abandons the plough, and divine because he prepares the way for God to enter.

The Overwhelming of the Lower Self by the Strength of the Individuality

In the mythic scenes where **Balarāma is seen intoxicated**, the surface may suggest indulgence—but metaphysically, **this is not drunkenness in the vulgar sense**. It is **divine intoxication**—the state that arises when the **lower self is overwhelmed by the descent of spiritual force from the Individuality.**

Just as **Noah's wine** and the mystical intoxication of the saints signify the inrushing of higher vibrations into the lower bodies, **Balarāma's "intoxication" is the result of his being a channel for Ananta—the endless serpent of cyclic power and cosmic rhythm.** When the lower nature is unprepared, this force disorients; when it is purified, it awakens bliss.

The Individuality is not passive. It transmits great waves of **truth, will, and sacred memory**. When this energy pours downward too suddenly, it can feel like a kind of disorientation, a loss of ego control. This is what mystics call divine madness, what prophets experience as ecstatic trembling.

Balarāma, as the **plough-bearer**, tills not just the soil of the soul, but also **opens channels between planes**. When this energy flows freely, it may cause the **ego-mind to reel**, unable to maintain its former constructs. In such moments, the soul appears drunk—but only because the **wine of divine energy** has replaced the waters of mundane thought.

Thus, Balarāma's "intoxication" is a **sacrament**, not a defect. It is **the experience of being overfilled with the force of the Monad**, of walking through the world **while remembering eternity**. It is the bliss that comes not from escape, but from the **inward flooding of the sacred current**—strong enough to uproot the world, gentle enough to grow a garden.

The Incarnate Self and the Divine Companion to the Strong Individuality

If **Balarāma** is the **Individuality**, the plough-bearing Monad that stabilizes and prepares the soul, then **Krishna** is the **Divine Self incarnate**, the radiant joy and wisdom of the higher Atman entering the world of form. Together, they are **not two separate beings**, but **the dual expression of the one Divine Journey**: Balarāma as **the vessel**, Krishna as **the indwelling flame**.

Raised together by **Nanda, the herdsman**, they are sheltered in the **purified mind**—a mind detached from ego and attuned to the sacred rhythm of nature. Nanda's name itself, meaning bliss or delight, is metaphysical shorthand for the **inner consciousness that has become receptive to divine presence**.

Balarāma walks beside Krishna not as servant, but as **equal complement**. His plough tills the field of the soul, his strength opens the furrows in which **Krishna, the Self, plants the seeds of divine knowing**. Without

Balarāma, Krishna has no field; without Krishna, Balarāma has no fruit.

In esoteric terms, Balarāma is the **individual line of memory** stretching back through incarnations, the carrier of karmic momentum, the strength of accumulated virtue. Krishna is the **moment of divine descent** when the Supreme says, "Now is the time to harvest." Their unity is the mystery of **preparation and presence**, **evolution and revelation**, **effort and grace**.

Thus, in every soul, these two walk together:

- **Balarāma as the one who has labored**, who has remembered, who has endured.

- **Krishna as the one who descends**, who illumines, who completes.

And in the moment of divine fulfillment, they are no longer two: they are **the soul becoming God, God recognizing the soul**, and the field of life blooming in between.

THE SACRED CULTIVATION OF THE SOUL BY THE INDIVIDUALITY

Ploughing, in spiritual symbolism, is far more than an agrarian metaphor—it is the **active work of the Individuality (Balarāma)** in preparing the field of the soul for divine realization. With his ploughshare in hand, **Balarāma is not merely a warrior, but a cosmic**

farmer, a tiller of karmic soil, whose role is to **break, soften, and ready the lower nature for divine implantation.**

The earth is not the planet—it is the **body, the emotions, the mind**, and all the subtle fields in which the soul must operate. These fields grow wild without cultivation. They are filled with stones of pride, roots of desire, and hardened by lifetimes of forgetfulness. **Balarāma enters this terrain with the plough**, slicing through ignorance, **turning the inner soil**, and **reorienting it toward the light**.

This act is not metaphorical—it is energetic and real. Every pain that turns us inward, every loss that humbles the ego, every insight that opens the heart—**these are furrows ploughed by the Individuality**, creating space where divine seeds can be planted.

In the Egyptian tradition, the Self says, "I plough therein; I reap therein." In Buddhist teaching, **wisdom is the plough, the Dharma the field, and Nirvana the harvest**. In all cases, **ploughing is initiation**—the moment the soul begins to cooperate with the evolutionary current rather than resist it.

Balarāma is the one who ploughs not with violence, but with vision. His furrows are not scars—they are the sacred lines in which the **light of Krishna** will soon take root. He does not plant the seed of God, but he makes sure that when the seed arrives, **it will find no resistance, no stones, no illusions too thick to grow through**.

He is the first act in the sacred ritual of incarnation. He is the force that **makes the soul ready**.

THE DIVINE SELF IN BATTLE AND THE EXPRESSION OF DHARMA THROUGH THE STRENGTH OF THE INDIVIDUALITY

If **Balarāma** is the **root strength of the soul**, the unwavering **Individuality**, then **Rama** is the **divine embodiment of that strength in action**—the incarnation of dharma, the **Self as king, warrior, and redeemer** moving through the fields that Balarāma has already prepared.

The two are not distinct but **reflective currents of the same spiritual reality**: Balarāma is the **eternal base of strength**, while Rama is that **strength manifested as sacred will**, embodied in the battlefield of life. Where Balarāma tills the inner soil, **Rama reclaims it**, liberating it from distortion (Rāvana), reuniting it with the soul's inner light (Sita), and **restoring divine sovereignty in the inner kingdom**.

Balarāma and Rama together form a **hidden dyad** within the soul:

- Balarāma is the **underground river**, carrying power, memory, and purpose through the ages.

- Rama is the **fountain that breaks the surface**, fully formed, radiant, and focused on right action.

Balarāma does not fight the battles—**he births the conditions** in which those battles must be fought. Rama steps forward to fulfill them.

And yet, Balarāma is always there—silent, strong, unseen—upholding Rama's vow, carrying his weight, **acting as the reservoir of will behind every divine strike.** He is the **interior flame of resilience** that refuses to collapse under the strain of exile, loss, or cosmic injustice. It is this inner monadic memory that **keeps Rama aligned with dharma**, even when everything outside calls him to abandon it.

When ancient battles are explored, **Balarāma will be recognized not as a bystander, but as the soul-force within Rama**, the one who held the line across incarnations, carried the sacred memory of Vishnu's rhythm, and tilled the path until the Divine could walk it.

Together, **Rama and Balarāma** show us that dharma is not a moment, but a journey; not a law, but a lineage—**rooted in the Individuality, flowering in the Self.**

The Silent Witness — Balarāma's Neutrality in the Kurukṣetra War

In the epoch of the great Kurukṣetra War, the world stood divided between the Pāṇḍavas and the Kauravas. Warriors from across realms chose sides, aligning with dharma or ambition. Yet, amidst this cosmic polarization, there existed a force that chose neither — **Balarāma**, the elder brother of Kṛṣṇa.

When approached by both factions, seeking his formidable strength, Balarāma declined participation. He embarked instead on a pilgrimage, distancing himself from the battlefield drenched in destiny and blood. His absence was not of indifference but of profound significance.

Metaphysical Interpretation:

Balarāma embodies the **Higher Mind**, the aspect of consciousness that observes without attachment, discerning without interference. In the theater of dualities — righteousness and unrighteousness, action and inaction — the Higher Mind remains **neutral**, understanding that the soul's journey transcends such binaries.

His choice to abstain from the war signifies the **state of equanimity** that the spiritual aspirant must cultivate. While the lower self engages in battles of desires and duties, the Higher Mind watches, guiding subtly but never imposing.

Balarāma's pilgrimage during the war symbolizes the **inner journey** one undertakes towards self-realization. Rather than being entangled in external conflicts, the seeker turns inward, seeking sanctity and understanding beyond the ephemeral victories and losses of the material realm.

Furthermore, his neutrality underscores the **principle of non-attachment**. Engagement in the world is necessary, but clinging to outcomes binds the soul. By neither supporting nor opposing, Balarāma exemplifies the balance between participation and detachment, urging the aspirant to act in the world without being of it.

In the grand narrative of the soul's evolution, Balarāma's stance during the Kurukṣetra War serves as a beacon for those treading the spiritual path. It teaches that beyond the tumultuous waves of worldly conflicts lies a serene shore of neutrality and wisdom. By aligning with the Higher Mind, one can navigate the dualities of existence with grace, understanding that true victory lies not in conquest but in inner harmony.

THE INFINITE CYCLE AND THE ETERNAL RHYTHM OF THE INDIVIDUALITY

Balarāma is said to be an incarnation of **Ananta**, the cosmic serpent, whose name means "endless." This is not a decorative title—it is a profound metaphysical declaration: **Balarāma is the embodiment of the eternal force that underlies continuity itself.** He is the **coiled memory of the cosmos**, the soul's persistent thread through all lifetimes.

The **serpent** has always symbolized **life-force**, **wisdom**, and **the cyclical movement of time**. But **Ananta** is no ordinary serpent—he is the **bed upon which Vishnu rests**, the foundation of all creation. Thus, Balarāma as Ananta represents the **Individuality as the coiled base upon which the Divine Self reclines before it awakens in the world**.

In the soul's inner temple, Balarāma is the **uncoiling spiral of divine evolution**. He holds the blueprint of all spiritual memory, all karmic design, all latent potential. He is the rhythm of return, the **timeless Monad who ploughs not just the field of one life, but of all lives**, keeping the soul's purpose intact across ages.

And just as **Ananta floats upon the ocean of primordial truth**, so too does Balarāma carry within him the **unspoken knowledge of where the soul has been and where it must go**. He is the strength of the soul that never forgets, even when the personality drowns in forgetfulness.

Metaphysically, this tells us that Balarāma is not simply strong—**he is enduring**. He is the **serpentine thread that spirals through every incarnation**, adapting, shaping, tilling, holding—until the time comes for Vishnu to rise, for Krishna to be born, for Rama to take the bow.

To call him Ananta is to say:
"He is always with you. He is the soul that never dies. He is the rhythm beneath your feet."

The Drunken Sage and the Secret Wisdom of the Individuality in Ecstatic Stillness

Silenus, the wise, drunken companion of Dionysus, is a figure cloaked in paradox—**intoxicated yet prophetic, foolish in appearance yet vast in vision**. In the same mystical light, **Balarāma mirrors Silenus**, not as a figure of excess, but as the **soul's inner sage—the Individuality flooded by divine current**, overflowing with the intoxication of spiritual remembrance.

Where Silenus staggers, he does so under the weight of truths too vast for the waking mind. And so it is with **Balarāma**, the one who has tilled and toiled, not only in the light, but also in **the deep subterranean chambers of the soul**, where language dissolves and only rhythm remains. His so-called "intoxication" is not inebriation—it is **ecstatic absorption into the higher vibrations of Self**, where **will and wisdom merge in silence**.

Silenus is often seen with music, wine, and sleep—but each of these is a metaphor:

- **Music** is the **harmonic intelligence** of the cosmos;

- **Wine** is the **divine current descending into the vessel**;

- **Sleep** is **withdrawal from the outer world to hear the inner one.**

These symbols apply equally to **Balarāma**. He is the **plough-bearer of the soul**, yet also the one who knows **when to surrender to the current of the Divine**. He does not speak often—but when he does, **he channels the deepest truths of the Monad**, born not of logic, but of resonance.

His strength is not mere discipline—it is also **capacity**: to hold, to withstand, and to let flow. The intoxicated state of Silenus and Balarāma alike reminds us that **when the soul becomes fully aligned with its source, it may appear foolish to the world—but inwardly, it becomes infinite**.

Thus, Balarāma as Silenus is the **inner mystic**, the **quiet flame**, the **soul that has seen too much to speak and too deeply to stand straight**—not because he has fallen, but because **he has merged.**

The Source of Divine Rhythm and the Womb of the Individuality

If **Balarāma** is the Individuality—the strong bearer of divine memory and spiritual will—then **Vishnu** is the **eternal pulse** from which that Individuality arises. **Balarāma is not separate from Vishnu—he is Vishnu's curvature into time**, the **loop of divine intention becoming continuity**, the **plough of preservation drawn across the fields of karma.**

Vishnu lies upon **Ananta**, the cosmic serpent of infinite recurrence, and Balarāma **is that serpent made active, that eternal rhythm walking the furrowed plains of incarnation**. Vishnu does not act directly—he dreams. He envisions. And from that dream, Balarāma emerges with **plough in hand**, to begin the **real work of soul-making.**

He is the **first expression of Vishnu's descent**, not yet divine incarnation (as in Krishna or Rama), but the **first preparation**: the formation of the causal body, the enduring ego, the sacred architecture through which **divine light may one day flow.**

Vishnu, as the **Preserver**, ensures **nothing essential is ever lost**. Balarāma, as his emanation, ensures **everything essential is cultivated.**
Where Vishnu watches over universes, **Balarāma tills the soul**.
Where Vishnu restores balance from the cosmos, **Balarāma restores rhythm within the self**.

And so, Balarāma is not just a fragment of Vishnu—**he is Vishnu's own stability made manifest**, the One who carries the burden of continuity, strength, and sacred effort through all lifetimes.

He is the promise that the soul will not be forsaken, that its field will be prepared, that even in confusion or despair, **someone within you remembers.**

He is Vishnu's presence **not as a thunderbolt**, but as a **ploughshare**—quiet, persistent, strong. He turns the soil until the Divine can walk it.

The Silent Strength That Carries God

Before Krishna sings and Rama slays, before the Self descends into light and battle, there is **a deeper silence** —a strength that has no need for praise, no longing for recognition. This is **Balarāma**, the enduring force beneath all divine embodiment—the **Monad in motion**, the **Divine Spark that remembers when all else forgets.**

He walks beside the Self, not in shadow, but in strength. He ploughs before the seed is planted. He tills the karma, bears the burden, and **carves the furrow into which God may descend.** He does not command thunder—he **moves the earth**, quietly, repeatedly, faithfully.

He is the Individuality that survives death, survives ego, survives time. He is the **thread that runs through lifetimes**, holding the line when all around is broken. And when he drinks the wine of spirit, he is not overcome—he is **expanded**, made radiant with the intoxication of sacred memory, overflowing with the rhythm of Ananta.

To know Balarāma is to remember that the journey is not in vain. That every effort, every lesson, every scar on the soul's field is part of a larger cultivation. That before the divine can act through you, there must be a self **strong enough to hold the divine.**

He is the plough and the serpent, the brother and the base, the joy behind silence and the strength behind grace.

And in the day of the great battle, when the Self rises to reclaim the soul, it will be Balarāma—the inner tiller—who has prepared the field.

He will not be seen. But he will be felt. And without him, there would be no incarnation.

The Metaphysical Identity of Rama — The Divine Self in Form

Rama is not merely a figure of virtue or myth. Rama is the projection of the eternal Self into the condition of form—not as an isolated avatar, but as the highest expression of divine order operating through individualized will. He is the Atmic flame made active in the realm of becoming, the Logos in motion, the principle of divine identity clothed in personal destiny. Rama is not to be understood merely through narrative or symbolism, but through his structural role within the metaphysical continuum: **he is the archetype of Selfhood aligned to cosmic law**, the instrument through which the Absolute begins its descent into individuality without separation from the eternal.

Rama exists because unity, though complete in itself, expresses its perfection through apparent division. He is the divine measure within that division. In Rama, the Self does not dissolve into the formless; it incarnates **with full**

memory of its source, bearing the burden of embodiment without succumbing to the distortion of separation. Where other souls arise in time as expressions of unfolding karma, Rama enters time as a clarifier of it. He is the **ideal human form**, not in the moral sense, but in the ontological: the human form as it was originally designed to carry the total vibration of spirit without distortion.

The presence of Rama is not a corrective to evil, but a reassertion of structure. In metaphysical terms, Rama is the **straight line**—the directional force of divine intelligence as it passes through the matrix of duality. He is not abstract light. He is focused will. Where the divine principle seeks to maintain balance through harmony, Rama does so through **form and function**, through task, role, and action.

This is why he must descend. The descent is not fall—it is appointment. It is the commitment of the eternal to participate in time, to redeem polarity not by avoiding it, but by mastering it from within.

Rama moves through a world bound by appearance, but he is never bound by it. Even his exile is not punishment—it is demonstration. His exile is the metaphysical reality that the true Self must pass through fragmentation before it can reintegrate the kingdom. His story is not linear history. It is the inner life of the soul when the soul begins to align itself with its higher nature. Sītā is not simply his consort—she is the **soul principle**, the subtle body of the Self, drawn into manifestation and then obscured by distortion. Her abduction is the soul's descent into captivity within the lower planes of inversion. Rama's war is not revenge. It is the **metaphysical return of divine order to the world of appearances**.

Rāvana, in this architecture, is not evil in the moral sense. He is the misalignment of power—a being of great force who has turned that force inward, severed from the law of truth. His many heads are the fragmented intellect, the scattered appetites, the proliferation of partial knowings cut off from their source. He is brilliant, but inverted. His strength lies in distortion, not in chaos, but in structure misused. The confrontation between Rama and Rāvana is therefore not between good and evil, but between aligned will and disordered brilliance—between the One who serves truth, and the one who serves self as truth.

Lakṣmaṇa is the extension of Rama's direction—**the movement of divine intention** into sharp, immediate action. He is precision, the faculty of sacred enforcement. Hanuman, by contrast, is the **bridge between spirit and matter**. He is the function of devotion in the metaphysical sense: the spiritual strength that carries the Self across the abyss. He does not act on desire. He acts as the **pure motor of divine loyalty**—the power of the soul aligned entirely to its source, undistracted, unwavering. Hanuman does not evolve; he is complete in his function. He is not climbing toward realization. He **is realization in movement**.

Lanka is the inversion of the soul's inner kingdom—a domain where strength is used to dominate, where intellect serves appetite, and where light is bent inward toward self-admiration. It is not merely a city. It is a state of consciousness—brilliant, orderly, powerful, but severed. Rama's war is therefore a return. Not conquest, but **reclamation**. Not destruction, but **purification of function**.

Rama's victory is not the triumph of righteousness. It is the reinstallation of divine intelligence as the principle behind all function. When Sītā is restored, the soul and the Self are reunited—not sentimentally, but structurally. The kingdom is not just regained; it is **re-consecrated**. The story does not end in peace. It ends in **alignment**—the final image is not happiness, but balance restored.

At the highest level, Rama is not a being. He is **a frequency of divine participation**. He is the affirmation that the Absolute not only sustains the cosmos but can enter it, move through it, act within it—without ceasing to be what it always is. Rama is the proof that the divine Self can walk through form, touch duality, engage with shadow, and remain whole. His presence does not reject form. It **redeems** it.

To contemplate Rama metaphysically is to contemplate the Self as structure. Not the dissolution of ego into light, but the transmutation of individuality into transparency. Rama is the Self when the Self is fully aligned with the Absolute yet fully available in action. He is the **architecture of sacred will**, the example not of escape from the world, but of mastery within it. The mind that sees Rama clearly no longer seeks transcendence as removal, but as **right participation**—where will, intelligence, form, and origin are one.

In this way, Rama is not just a god among men, but **the eternal design of divine identity made visible**—the way in which the Real passes into appearance without distortion, and returns to itself without loss. He is the metaphysical self-awakening within form—lawful, luminous, and whole.

RAMA CHAPTER 3

SITA - Alignment with the Buddhic emotion

The **Atma Plane** is the highest field of spiritual manifestation accessible to the soul in the current evolutionary cycle. It is not a location in space but a **state of divine fusion**, where the **power and love aspects of Deity converge** in radiant equilibrium. At this level, the Self no longer perceives reality through fragmentation—it beholds all things through the lens of **unity, purpose, and timeless motion**.

This is the realm of the **Second Logos**, the **Higher Self**, not yet clothed in form, but already reaching toward incarnation. Here, the Self is not active in personality or emotional life—it is the **silent architect**, brooding upon the deep, shaping intention from the cosmic field of pure being.

From the Atma Plane descends the **creative Word**, not as a sound, but as a **command of harmony**. This is the level from which archetypes are breathed into existence, and **forces below begin to turn in rhythm with divine intent.** The Atma Plane is not the force—it is the **ruling of forces**. As a rider steers a horse without pulling the reins, so too does Atma govern the lower energies—not with effort, but with presence.

At this level, **spiritual individuality merges with cosmic law**. The soul becomes a carrier of divine volition, not merely aspiring to truth, but **becoming the expression of truth itself**. The Atma Plane is the throne of this sovereign potential—a reality only touched when the soul has shed all sense of separation.

To dwell upon this plane, even momentarily, is to stand in the innermost sanctuary of the Self, where **no thought exists, but only knowing**, no action remains, but only being. It is the **first place of divine fusion**, where the Father and Son, source and spark, are no longer separate —**but one flame.**

The Buddhic Function — The Soul's Inner Alchemy and the Ladder of Sacred Ascent

The **Buddhic Function** is the **inner alchemical process** by which the **lower nature of the soul is transmuted into its divine potential**. It is the sacred operation of the **higher emotional intelligence**, the luminous faculty that does not destroy the passions but **redeems them**, refining the soul's crude desires into radiant love, intuition, and wisdom.

This function is not an external act—it is an **invisible current within the soul** that awakens when the personality begins to long for more than fleeting pleasure. It begins as a **vague unrest**, a nameless dissatisfaction with lower attachments. But in truth, this yearning is the

voice of Buddhi, the higher principle calling the soul back toward its origin.

Buddhi does not push—it magnetizes. It sends **vibrations from above**, subtle yet powerful, that begin to shape the mental and emotional bodies from within. The higher mind—especially its fourth sub-plane, the realm of abstract ideals—becomes a **receptive mirror**, and through this mirror, **Buddhi transmits its light** into the structures of the lower self.

This transmission creates an **inner reciprocity**: as the lower self becomes more refined, **it can receive more of Buddhi's energy**, accelerating its transformation. This is the **ladder of transmutation**, built not by outer force, but by **inner resonance**. Buddhi acts like the **sun to a seed**—it does not tear the soil, but it draws the flower upward by radiating what it is.

In this way, the Buddhic Function **governs evolution from behind the veil**. It does not impose—it **rules by harmony**, shaping the soul like a potter's hand, guiding not by command but by vibration. Its fruits are the **higher emotions**: courage, compassion, devotion, joy without cause. These are not reactions—they are **emanations**, the soul's own answer to the touch of its higher Self.

To awaken the Buddhic Function is to enter the path of **martyrs, saints, sages, and lovers of truth**—for once touched by Buddhi, the soul **cannot serve illusion again**. It begins to rise, led not by force, but by a **vision too beautiful to ignore.**

The Buddhic Plane — The Womb of Divine Realization and the Garden of the Higher Self

The **Buddhic Plane** is the **first true home of the soul in its divine unfolding**—the field of consciousness where the **Higher Self first takes form**, not in body, but in **essence, light, and archetype**. It is the plane just above the mental world, yet it is **not a realm of thought**—it is a **realm of knowing, feeling, and being**, all fused into a single radiant awareness.

It is here that the **soul's higher causal body** resides, the temple of its noblest qualities, virtues, and divine patterns. The Buddhic Plane is not visible to ordinary consciousness, for it does not express through language or sensation. It speaks through **presence**, through **higher emotions** like compassion, joy, harmony, and deep inner stillness—what ancient texts call the **"fruit of the Spirit."**

Unlike the lower planes, the Buddhic is not shaped by personal effort. It is **not built—it is revealed**. It already exists within the soul as a divine potential, and **as the lower nature is purified, the soul begins to ascend into it**, not by climbing, but by **remembering**.

This plane is also the **domain of spiritual prototypes**—the perfect patterns of all things that grow. Minerals, plants, animals, and humans all have their **ideal forms reflected here**, like sacred blueprints. This is why the Buddhic Plane is described as the **garden** or **Eden** of the soul—**the realm before division**, before duality, where the essence of all life sings in harmony.

When the soul fully enters the Buddhic Plane, it begins to **merge with its higher destiny**. The separations between "I" and "you," "self" and "world," begin to dissolve. Compassion is no longer a virtue—it is the **natural state of being**. Knowledge becomes intuition. Choice becomes dharma. **Emotion becomes light.**

This is also the **first domain into which the Higher Self descends during incarnation**, meaning it is the **original descent point of divine intelligence** into the world of form. And it is the **final ascent point**, the place to which the soul returns in its perfected state—whole, radiant, and woven back into the divine song.

To touch the Buddhic Plane is to remember your origin. To live from it is to become the light you once sought.

Sītā — The Radiant Soul-Light and the Sacred Emotion-Nature of the Self

Sītā, the consort of Rāma, is far more than a wife in myth—she is the **soul's divine essence**, the **buddhic emotion-nature**, the **living stream of higher feeling** that flows alongside the Higher Self through incarnation. She is **the soul's purity before distortion**, the part of us born of sacred soil, taken into exile, but never defiled.

She emerges not from a womb, but from a **furrow in the earth**—a powerful metaphor that reveals her nature as **fruit of the soul's tillage**, born only when the lower nature has been ploughed and prepared by the work of the Individuality. She is the **buddhic flower** that blooms from the transmutation of the emotional body—**the soul's reward for its fidelity to truth**.

Sītā is not passive. She is the **guiding presence within**, the **silent knowing that draws the Self forward**. When she is abducted by Rāvana (the desire-principle), it signifies how **the soul's light can be captured by illusion**, how higher emotions become trapped in the fortress of egoic craving. Yet even in captivity, Sītā does not yield. Her light is constant. Her devotion unwavering.

She belongs to Rāma because she is **his mirror**. Where Rāma is the Higher Self, Sītā is the **buddhic reflection**—the part of the soul that still feels truth, even when surrounded by falsehood. She is the **quiet pulse of the Divine Feminine**, the inner Lakshmi, the **vibration of harmony and intuition** that never forgets its origin, even in the darkest exile.

Her trial by fire is her transfiguration. As she **invokes Agni**, the god of fire, she steps into the sacred flames not to be judged, but to be **revealed**. And from that flame comes the gods, the old king, and the final revelation: **Sītā is Lakshmi. Rāma is Nārāyana. And together they are the divine pair, inseparable, eternal, whole.**

This moment is the soul's great unveiling. The **buddhic nature ascends**, purified and transmuted, and in doing so, **awakens the full realization of the Self as God**. The ideals—those gods within—are energized. The emotional body no longer reacts—it radiates. The **buddhic**

light lifts the consciousness to the atmic plane, and there, the Divine Father and Son become **One Truth-Reality**.

Thus, **Sītā is the soul's light of devotion, its sacred memory, its hidden strength**. She is the part of us that never forgets love, even when love is exiled. She is the divine feminine force that walks silently beside the Self, waiting for the moment when the soul becomes whole again.

To know Sītā is to awaken the **buddhic flame** within.
To love her is to feel the Self's deepest longing: not for conquest, but for reunion.
And to reclaim her is to remember that the soul is not earned—it is already yours.
It waits only to be liberated.

Erectheus and the Transmutation of the Buddhic Emotion-Nature

In the deeper cosmology of the soul's evolution, the being known as Erectheus is not simply mythic. He is the **metaphysical archetype of the philosophic intellect**, born not of pure spirit, but of **disciplined substance**—symbolized by the ploughed earth. This earth is not base matter; it is lower nature that has been prepared through alignment, culture, and inner rectification. And what nurtures this philosophic emergence is not intellect itself, but the **descending ray of the buddhic light**, the higher wisdom principle symbolized by Athena.

This framework provides a crucial insight into the real nature of **Sītā**.

Sītā is not the soul in its raw emotional form. She is the **buddhic emotion-nature**—an elevated and transmuted field of consciousness that reflects the **principle of Buddhi** in its alliance with the **Higher Self**, Rama. She is not formed by desire, but by the **refinement of emotion through spiritual discipline**, just as the philosophic intellect is formed by the conditioning of the ploughed earth. In this context, Sītā is not the ground; she is what the ground, when properly cultivated, allows to emerge: a vessel through which the **buddhic fire may dwell**.

Erectheus, as symbol, reveals that intellect becomes fit for higher reception only when disciplined by structure and nurtured from above. So too does Sītā illustrate that emotion becomes a carrier of divine reality only when refined by devotion and made transparent to spirit. **She is the purified receptivity** that allows the divine ideals (the gods) to become operative—just as the philosophic intellect, once elevated, gains access to the archetypal realms.

The alignment is precise.

Where Erectheus rides the chariot of four horses—signifying mastery over the four planes of being—Sītā enters the flame, not to be consumed, but to reveal that her nature is already harmonized. She is not being tested; she is being **unveiled**. Her immersion in fire is not an ordeal—it is a demonstration of the soul's Buddhic maturity: no longer reactive, no longer seeking, but fully aligned with the Real.

And in this unveiling, the **Divine Son and the Divine Father are revealed as One**, and Sītā is recognized not as the object of devotion, but as the **living principle through which devotion itself is transfigured**. She is not the goal of the journey—she is its **capacity**. She is the soul made radiant through discipline, the refined vessel through which divine law becomes perceptible. In the presence of such Buddhic light, Rama's full identity is revealed—not as hero, but as **Nārāyaṇa**, the Eternal Self.

Thus, Erectheus and Sītā converge—not through shared narrative, but through **structural function**. Both represent the transmutation of nature by discipline, the nourishment from above by Buddhi, and the **revealing of divine identity** through inner refinement. One is masculine, emerging as philosophic clarity; the other, feminine, manifesting as devotional fire. But in both, the same law is shown:

Only that which is prepared and lifted can receive the Real.

Fire — The Sacred Revealer, the Trial of Purity, and the Elemental Mirror of the Soul

In the climactic moment of her story, **Sītā steps into fire** —not as punishment, but as **sacrament**. Fire, in the metaphysical tradition, is not destruction but **revelation**. It is the element that consumes illusion, separates shadow from essence, and **lays bare the true nature of all things.** To pass through fire and remain is to prove one's divinity.

Sītā's entry into the flames of Agni is the transmutation of the soul's emotional nature. In this act, the **buddhic essence is tested by the sacred flame of will**, stripped of all outer form and freed from distortion. Fire does not create truth—it reveals it. And in Sītā's case, **what is revealed is Lakshmi**, the radiant embodiment of divine love and abundance.

This moment corresponds to a profound spiritual law: the **lower emotions must pass through the fire of higher will** in order to become instruments of light. Only through this burning away does the soul rise from the emotional plane to the **buddhic and ultimately atmic realms**. Sītā's fire-trial is the soul's own journey through purification: it is the **refinement of love through suffering**, the revelation of purity through silence.

But more than just a symbol of trial, **Fire is the sacred witness**. Agni, as the guardian of truth, acts as both **judge and liberator**. The fire does not burn Sītā because it recognizes her nature. This is the secret meaning: **when**

the soul is aligned with its essence, even fire becomes an ally.

Thus, Sītā's relationship to fire is not fear—it is fulfillment. She becomes fire's mirror, reflecting not destruction, but sanctity.

And so, in every soul, there comes a moment where we must step into our own fire—not to prove we are worthy, but to let all that is false fall away.

The Womb of the Earth and the Sacred Channel of Divine Emergence

Sītā is not born from flesh, but from a furrow—a sacred groove carved into the earth by the plough. This is not mere poetic ornamentation. It is a **metaphysical cipher**, revealing that Sītā is the **fruit of cultivation**, the **buddhic essence of the soul** brought forth only after deep inner labor. She is **the soul's harvest**, born of soil turned by the Individuality (Balarāma), emerging from the **furrowed field of the purified self**.

The **furrow** is both **wound and womb**—a rupture in the hardened earth, made open to receive the higher current. In the same way, the soul's lower nature must be broken open through trial, humility, and longing for truth. Only then can Sītā—**the divine feminine light of the higher emotion-nature—rise like a flower from the soil of transmuted selfhood**.

And it is no accident that the plough that made this furrow belongs to Balarāma, the archetype of the Individuality. For it is he who prepares the inner terrain through karma, sacrifice, and strength. Sītā's birth is thus **the result of soul cultivation**, proof that the **lower nature has become fertile enough to carry divine grace**.

The furrow also speaks to **alignment**—it is a straight path drawn across the chaotic earth, a symbol of the soul's readiness to receive **higher vibration in structured form.** Just as the plough sets the direction, the furrow receives it, and **life begins.**

So Sītā is not just born of the earth—**she is born of the earth rightly prepared**.

She is the feminine principle that **waits not in the sky, but in the soil**, the light that will not come until the soul is ready, until the field has been tilled, and the heart made soft.

She is the fulfillment of sacred tillage.
She is the soul's hidden seed, at last brought to bloom.

The Devoted Bridge Between Self and Soul, the Messenger of Sacred Reunion

Hanuman, the devoted servant of Rāma, is not merely a figure of strength and loyalty—he is, metaphysically, **the awakened mind in service to the Higher Self**, the

inner force of devotion and discrimination that bridges the gap between **Rāma (the Higher Self)** and **Sītā (the buddhic soul-light)** when they are separated by illusion.

In the metaphysical landscape, Hanuman represents **buddhi-manas**—the purified mind that is no longer allied with lower desire, but instead turned wholly toward the soul's inner truth. His leap across the ocean to reach Sītā in Lanka is the **mind transcending the sea of samsara**, crossing the illusion of separation to reclaim the **sacred feminine within**.

Sītā, exiled and captive in the fortress of Rāvana (desire), cannot be reached through force or intellect alone. Only **devotion, humility, and direct perception** can find her. Hanuman is this principle—**the fearless inner agent of reunion**, driven by nothing but pure love for the Self and reverence for the soul.

When Hanuman finds Sītā, he does not demand, lecture, or rescue by force. He **places the ring of Rāma in her hands**—a symbol of memory, of eternal union, of unbroken love. This reveals the deepest teaching: **the Self and the Soul are never truly separate**. The illusion of separation is powerful, but the devotion of the purified mind can **carry the signature of the Self into the depths of the psyche**, and reawaken the light that was hidden.

Sītā receives Hanuman as a **reminder of her divinity**, a messenger from her beloved, and in that moment, she is no longer merely a captive—**she becomes the queen of her own inner kingdom once more**.

Thus, Hanuman is not just the servant—he is the **agent of restoration**, the embodiment of what happens when the mind becomes the handmaiden of the soul, not its captor.

In the soul's journey, Hanuman appears when the fire of devotion becomes stronger than the pull of illusion. And in that moment, **Sītā is found again—not in a distant realm, but in the garden of the heart.**

THE DIVINE FEMININE AS RADIANT ORDER, SOULFUL ABUNDANCE, AND THE UNSHAKABLE CORE OF SĪTĀ

Lakshmi, the goddess of beauty, abundance, and spiritual harmony, is not merely a consort to the divine—she is the **very pattern of balance**, the **fractal of divine symmetry** woven into the soul. When the gods appear and declare that **Sītā is Lakshmi**, they do not elevate her—they reveal her.

Sītā has always been Lakshmi. She is **the soul's hidden wealth**, the sacred light that does not dazzle, but sustains. Where Lakshmi is the **cosmic empress of equilibrium**, Sītā is **that principle manifest within the individual soul**—the **buddhic resonance of devotion, grace, and inner plentitude**. She is not wealth as possession—**she is wealth as spiritual presence**, as the fullness of the divine feminine known only by those who have endured exile.

As Lakshmi, Sītā represents the **principle of inner sacred order**—the alignment of the soul with the harmonious law of the cosmos. Even in Lanka, even in captivity, she does not collapse into despair. Her grace is not diminished because her outer freedom is gone—**her inner wholeness remains intact**, untouched by illusion. This is the secret of Lakshmi: **true abundance cannot be imprisoned**.

And when Sītā passes through fire, she does not become Lakshmi—**the fire merely reveals that she always was**. Just as gold is purified in flame, her true form shines through the trial. She is Lakshmi not only in peace, but in exile, in suffering, in silence.

She teaches us that the soul's feminine essence does not abandon us—it waits. It sits beneath the ash, radiant, unwavering, ready to rise when the Self returns.

Sītā, as Lakshmi, is the **restoration of spiritual equilibrium**. Her reunion with Rāma is not just the return of love—it is the return of divine order. Together, they symbolize the soul and Self reunited, the **masculine and feminine within us restored**, the golden balance reestablished.

In every human heart, Lakshmi waits as Sītā—
Not demanding attention, but offering wholeness.
Not seeking validation, but radiating truth.

The Fortress of Illusion, the Psyche's Inverted Palace, and the Exile of the Soul's Light

Lanka, the golden city ruled by Rāvana, is not simply a geographical setting—it is a **metaphysical symbol of the lower psyche** when it is ruled by the **desire-mind**, by false sovereignty, by fragmented power divorced from truth. It is the soul's **inverted palace**, where beauty exists without balance, where knowledge is present without wisdom, and where the **soul's highest light (Sītā)** is held captive within the fortress of distorted will.

When **Sītā is taken to Lanka**, it is not merely abduction—it is the **exile of the buddhic soul-light into the domain of ego**, where desire sits on the throne. Lanka represents the **inner kingdom when governed by the wrong ruler**, where the masculine principle (Rāvana) has lost alignment with the Divine (Rāma) and instead seeks to possess the feminine (Sītā) for its own glorification.

This captivity is not a loss of purity, but a **concealment of truth**. Sītā remains untouched—not because she is defended by walls, but because **her light is self-radiant**. Even in Lanka, she resides within herself. Her captivity is symbolic of the inner human condition, where **the soul's true emotion-nature is trapped beneath layers of craving, ambition, and illusion**, but still waiting, still watching.

Lanka is filled with gold, towers, pleasures—**a false paradise** that masks its inner distortion. This is the soul under the rule of Rāvana: externally impressive, inwardly misaligned. It is the mind seduced by power, cut off from love.

And so the journey of the Higher Self (Rāma) is to **reclaim Lanka**—not just to defeat the desire-principle, but to **restore divine order** to the soul's inner world. To make the **city of illusion** into a **temple of truth**. But that reclamation is not possible until **Sītā is remembered**, until the **light of the soul is found again** in the innermost garden of the psyche.

For wherever your Sītā has been taken—
The divine waits not in rage, but in return.

Lanka teaches us that the soul's light may be exiled, but never extinguished.
That even in the palace of desire, the voice of purity can still be heard.

NĀRĀYANA — The Cosmic Self Revealed, the Infinite Lover, and the Union of Divine Masculine and Feminine

When the gods reveal to Rāma, after Sītā's trial by fire, that he is **Nārāyana**, it is not a promotion—it is a remembrance. **Nārāyana** is the **cosmic Self**, the **eternal masculine current of divine will, preservation, and harmony** that flows through all creation. He is the **divine motion within form**, the aspect of God that moves into manifestation to restore sacred balance.

To say that Rāma is Nārāyana is to declare that the Higher Self is not merely a soul's guide, but a **fully divine expression of cosmic order**. And to say that Sītā is Lakshmi is to declare that she is not merely his consort, but **his eternal counterpart**, the **buddhic soul-light that reflects his power in beauty, grace, and sacred feeling**.

Together, Nārāyana and Lakshmi represent the **indivisible unity of spirit and soul**, of masculine and feminine, of will and love. Their separation was illusion. Their reunion is not a conclusion—it is a **return to eternal truth**. The soul and the Self were never meant to be apart. Their exile was the myth; **their unity is the reality behind all realities**.

In metaphysical terms, this reunion occurs on the **Atma Plane**—the highest realm of conscious being in this cycle of evolution—where the **Father and Son**, the spark and the source, become **one luminous flame**. On this plane, the soul no longer seeks. It knows. It remembers. It becomes.

And here, the name **Nārāyana** reveals its deeper meaning:

- Nāra (man, soul)
- Ayana (resting place, goal, home)

Nārāyana is "He in whom the souls take refuge." And Sītā, the soul-light, returns to him—not in submission, but in sacred partnership. Their embrace is the **fusion of**

polarity into unity, the completion of the inner journey from exile to embodiment.

The soul is never lost.
The Self is never far.
They were only playing the cosmic drama of forgetting and remembering, of longing and return.

And when Sītā and Rāma are revealed as Lakshmi and Nārāyana, the soul awakens to this secret:
We are not only made in the image of God—we are the reunion of its parts.

THE EMBODIED SELF, THE UPHOLDER OF DHARMA, AND THE DIVINE CONSORT OF THE SOUL'S RADIANT LIGHT

Rāma is not simply a king, a hero, or even an avatar—he is the **Higher Self** incarnate, the **divine will manifesting in the world to uphold sacred law**, to restore balance, to retrieve what was lost. And he does not act alone—his journey, his trials, his very awakening are **incomplete without Sītā**, for she is the **buddhic soul-light that reveals who he truly is**.

When Sītā is exiled, Rāma is incomplete. When she is taken, **he is not merely angered—he is diminished**. For the Self without the Soul is will without warmth, action without intuition. Their separation is the dramatization of the soul's own split—between the outer actor and the inner essence, between form and feeling, between dharma and devotion.

And yet, it is **through Sītā's exile** that Rāma's full nature is revealed. Only through losing her does he discover the depth of his divine identity. Only by pursuing her does he come into contact with Hanuman (devoted mind), confront Rāvana (egoic desire), and fulfill his **higher destiny as Nārāyana**. Thus, Sītā is not only his beloved—**she is his initiation**.

In this way, Rāma's devotion to Sītā mirrors the Self's eternal longing for reunion with the Soul. He does not dominate her. He seeks her. He remembers her. And when she steps into fire and emerges unchanged, **Rāma is transformed**—not because he gains her, but because he sees **what she always was**.

Their reunion is not romantic—it is **cosmic**. It is the union of Atma and Buddhi, of Self and Soul, of divine masculine and divine feminine, each **reflecting and completing the other**, each carrying the flame of the One Reality in a different tone.

In truth, Rāma never left her.
And Sītā was never truly lost.
They were playing the sacred game of separation—so that, through the fire, they might remember **what cannot be broken.**

In you, Rāma is the voice of dharma.
In you, Sītā is the light of soul-truth.
And their story is **your own return to wholeness**.

Closing Reflection — The Soul's Light That Waits in Silence

Sītā is the sacred essence within you that was never born of flesh but drawn forth from the furrowed field of your becoming. She is not just a character in a story—she is the **living memory of your higher nature**, the quiet pulse of love and purity that remains unshaken even when surrounded by illusion.

She is the **buddhic flame**—the soul's soft but radiant light, untouched by time, hidden beneath the layers of desire and suffering. And though she may seem lost at times, exiled, taken, or forgotten, she is never extinguished. Even in Lanka, even in fire, **Sītā remembers**. She waits, she prays, and she sustains the promise that **what is divine cannot be possessed, only reclaimed**.

Through her journey we remember that the soul is not weak because it feels—it is strong because it endures. That purity is not the absence of struggle, but the refusal to betray one's essence in the face of it. Sītā does not fight with swords—she fights with silence, with patience, with the power of **being aligned with the truth of who she is**.

And when Rāma returns—not just as man, but as Nārāyana—the Self sees the Soul not as shadow, but as **the mirror of its own divinity**. Their reunion is not just a marriage—it is the moment the soul remembers that **love, wisdom, will, and grace were never separate at all**.

In every sacred being, there is a Sītā—
A light hidden in soil, held in silence,
Tested by fire, revealed by love.
She is not waiting for rescue—
She is waiting to be remembered.

And once remembered,
She transforms the heart into a throne,
And the Self into a king.

RAMA CHAPTER 4

INDRA, THE THOUSAND-EYED GOD

A Metaphysical Profile of the Divine Will in the Soul:

Indra is the inner principle of Divine Will that emerges when the soul turns its gaze upward—toward the Highest. It is not a passive force, but a conscious devotion and driving power that moves through the higher faculties of being. It is the steadfast, all-perceiving current within the soul that seeks union with the Supreme by climbing upward through the mountain of inward striving. Indra does not represent mere action or desire—it is that awakened earnestness of the soul that has chosen to devote itself to spiritual ascent.

To speak of Indra as "Thousand-Eyed" is to signify the complete awakening of inner sight across the many layers of consciousness. It is not a physical seeing, but a supreme perception—where the Divine Will surveys all levels of being and penetrates every plane, seeking to bring the light of the Spirit into manifestation. The eyes of Indra are the thousand awakened petals of perception, scattered across the soul's landscape like luminous seeds of purpose.

Yet this exalted force, this luminous Will, must pass through the resistance of the soul's lower planes. As the soul descends into the denser spheres of desire and manifestation, the divine faculties of Indra seem to be veiled or even lost. The "people" of the soul—the unrefined thoughts, instincts, and emotional tendencies—rise up and appear to mock or nullify the presence of the Divine Will. These untransformed forces see only their own small dominion and attempt to erase all trace of Indra's higher sovereignty.

But Indra is never truly destroyed. It is hidden, withdrawn, or obscured, waiting in the high sanctum of the spiritual mind until the soul is ready to receive it again. Power is transferred, not lost—moving through higher channels (the Sakyas) into the lower being. This descent is necessary, for only through embodiment can the Divine Will eventually rise again, purified through experience, to lead the soul onward.

Indra is also the keeper of purity and the giver of divine riches—not of wealth as the world knows it, but of higher forces: insight, illumination, discernment, strength of will, and unwavering devotion to truth. These treasures are stored not in the outer world but in the kingdom of the inner Self. The rise of Indra within the soul is the rise of spiritual government over the senses.

Indra's path is not isolated. It is part of the greater architecture of evolution, woven into the upward journey of the soul. It is a gatekeeper, a guardian of entry into higher wisdom, and a luminous archetype of the Will of God as it seeks to descend and then reascend through the structure of the human being.

Indra, then, is the awakened force of spiritual determination. It is the soul's choice to devote itself wholly to the Highest—refusing the illusions of desire and thoughtlessness. It is the One-Eyed King whose thousand eyes have seen the path to God and who guides the Self along it, no matter how many times he must be buried by the crowd of lesser instincts and raised again by the breath of spiritual discipline.

THE PATH OF THE GODS
The Sacred Road of Indra's Ascent

If Indra is the sovereign principle of Divine Will in the soul, then **Devayana** is the path through which that Will travels upward toward its Source. It is the sacred ascent of consciousness, the return of the soul to the higher planes after it has awakened to truth, discerned good from evil, and taken up the labor of spiritual unfolding.

Devayana is the movement of the **Divine Spark**—the monad of life—once it has passed beyond mere form and entered into the current of inner becoming. As the Self begins to rise, it moves through stages, each one governed by spiritual energies: the **force of transformation (Agni)**, the **wind of intellect (Vayu)**, the **illumination of truth (Varuna)**, and the **steadfast will and vision of the Highest (Indra and Prajāpati)**. These stages do not represent locations but inner thresholds of mastery—inner temples where certain aspects of the soul must awaken and submit to the Divine.

Indra, on this sacred path, stands as a **living power among these forces**—the unwavering torch of devotion, holding fast to spiritual purpose even when the soul falters or descends. As the Will climbs through the ladder of light, it passes through the plane of devotion, the plane of wisdom, and at last reaches **Brahman**, the undivided ocean of Pure Spirit. Here, Indra's long journey concludes —not in isolation, but in union.

What's most striking about Devayana is its demand that the Self undergo **inner purification and self-governance**. Each ascending step refines the faculties, widens the soul's horizons, and compels it to release attachment to darkness. This is where Indra reclaims his throne—not by conquering from without, but by rising from within.

Just as in the Rigveda the soul is said to "travel the way of the gods," Devayana reveals how the **inner Will (Indra)** matures through incarnation, sheds ignorance, and ascends by degrees into perfect clarity. Thus, Devayana is not just a metaphysical pathway—it is the very **channel through which Indra rises to lordship within**.

Indra is both walker and guardian of this sacred way. He is the Will that steps forward in faith and devotion, and he is also the unwavering sentinel who makes sure the soul stays true to the course. Without Devayana, Indra's thousand eyes remain blind. With it, they open into radiant stars guiding the soul's return.

The Fuel of Indra's Fire

If Devayana is the path, then **Devotion** is the **inner flame** that moves the soul forward on that path. Indra, as a symbol of Divine Will, is not an impersonal force of ambition or conquest. He is the **embodied will-to-serve**, forged in the fire of surrender to something higher. His many eyes do not merely watch—they witness with reverence. His strength is not self-derived—it is summoned through love of the Highest.

Devotion is the soul's **act of consecration**, the point where the ego steps aside so that the Higher Self may lead. It is the relinquishment of self-seeking and personal desire in favor of truth, goodness, and love. When the heart turns fully to the Divine, the Will (Indra) becomes clarified and aligned. No longer a flickering flame tossed by emotional winds, it becomes a **pillar of light**, unwavering in direction.

And here is the mystery: devotion is not weakness—it is power channeled through surrender. It is in this holy act that Indra rises to the "lordship of the gods," not through might, but through **earnestness**. Devotion is the gravity that pulls all higher spiritual qualities into form. It is how Truth becomes incarnate. It is how Light is sustained in darkness.

This is why Indra cannot be separated from Devotion. He is Devotion made active. His strength does not lie in dominance, but in **resolute loyalty to the Highest**, even when the lower world mocks, forgets, or annihilates every trace of the sacred. Devotion makes Indra immune to thoughtlessness—it gives him eyes that never close and a will that never breaks.

In this way, devotion becomes the inner compass of Indra's sovereignty. Without it, his thousand eyes go dim, and the Will dissolves into self-serving cunning. But with it, the soul becomes indestructible—a throne of Divine Will seated in the purified heart.

THE DOORKEEPERS — Indra and Pragāpati

A Metaphysical Layer within the Indra Profile

In the soul's ascent through the sacred halls of inner transformation, the archetypal figures of **Indra** and **Pragāpati**emerge as the **Doorkeepers of the Hall of Brahman**. They represent the final threshold between the conditioned self and the infinite expanse of pure spirit. These two forces stand at the portal not as guards in opposition, but as divine sentinels of Will and Wisdom, testing the soul's readiness to pass beyond form and duality into the absolute reality of Brahman.

Indra, in this context, no longer represents merely active spiritual will or vigilance, but becomes the distilled Will of the Supreme itself—focused, refined, and unwavering. Pragāpati, likewise, stands for the Divine Wisdom that creates and sustains both matter and spirit, the sacred architect whose sacrifice built the bridge between worlds. Together, they are the dual keys: the Will to ascend and the Wisdom to perceive the path.

In the **Kaushitaki Upanishad**, the moment the soul approaches these Doorkeepers, it is said that **they "run away from him"**. This is not rejection, but transfiguration. When the soul has fulfilled the necessary inner alchemy—when its lower nature has been transmuted, and its center of identity has shifted from ego to essence—these two forces are no longer required as outer conditioning factors. They dissolve because their task is complete: the soul has become self-ruling in Will and self-revealing in Wisdom. It now walks not toward Brahman, but as Brahman.

The **Doorkeepers**, therefore, are not literal obstacles but inner initiators—symbols of those supreme qualities which must be firmly seated within the aspiring Self before liberation becomes possible. They stand at the close of the lesser path and the beginning of the Greater. To pass them is to leave behind all external striving and enter the sanctuary where dualities fade, where Truth is not known but **embodied**, and where the Divine no longer speaks from without—but rises from within.

Lower Nature vs. the Higher Self

The term "People" in the esoteric context does not refer to individuals in the conventional sense, but rather symbolizes the **undeveloped instincts**, **emotional reactions**, and **natural impulses** of the lower mind. These "people" are not yet refined by the light of the higher consciousness. They represent the psychic crowd within—the emotional multitude and thoughtless masses of sensation, urge, and habitual pattern.

In the context of **Indra**, who symbolizes the **Divine Will**, **perception**, and **spiritual steadfastness**, the "People" appear as the lower attributes which threaten to **annihilate** or obscure the higher spiritual vision. As the text indicates, "Yonder Indra has been utterly annihilated by the people..." This means that once the lower faculties seize control of the inner temple, the **brilliance and clarity of Divine Will** is swallowed in the fog of instinctual response, conformity, emotional bondage, and spiritual distraction.

Yet paradoxically, these same "people" are also raw material. They are to be **disciplined and transmuted**, like unruly citizens in the kingdom of the Self who must be brought into the service of Truth. When properly harmonized by the higher spiritual forces (Indra), these lower tendencies become tools of **manifestation**, rather than forces of obscuration.

The metaphysical Christ, in the excerpted verse, turns to the lamenting crowd and says, "Weep not for me, but for yourselves." This reflects the Higher Self's address to the emotional self: you grieve externally for the loss of divine qualities, yet do not realize that your own internal state—your submission to bondage, tradition, and blind instinct—is the true tragedy. The Self mourns not because it has descended, but because the soul does not recognize what it has lost by turning away from it.

Thus, in Indra's case, "People" serve as a symbol of **that which must be overcome** or **purified**, in order for Divine Will and earnestness to rule again. The more attention is paid to the many "people" within—the multitude of voices, moods, opinions, and subconscious habits—the less space is available for the thousand-eyed vision of Indra, the overseeing Divine Intelligence.

The spiritual Singers

The Spiritual Monads Descending from the Higher Planes

In the metaphysical schema, the **Singers**, or **Pious Singers**, are not merely beings who vocalize devotion but represent **spiritual monads—divine sparks** descending from the **atma plane** into human experience. These monads, referred to as the **Maruts** in Vedic tradition, are radiant fragments of the Eternal Spirit who, in harmony and bliss, choose to enter into the cycle of manifestation. Their "singing" is not a literal melody but a **vibration of divine joy**, a **tone of spiritual purpose**—a frequency through which divine will and truth express themselves on lower planes.

In the context of **Indra**, these Singers serve as **echoes of the Divine Will**. They yearn for the "light of heaven"—the highest truth and awareness symbolized by Indra himself. Their songs are directed toward the Giver of Wealth, not material riches, but the **wealth of Spirit**, the full radiant glory of divine power, love, and wisdom. Thus, they are **spiritual heralds**, flowing downward from the heavens with the purpose of infusing the soul with sacred energy and remembrance.

These Singers participate in the drama of the soul's descent and ascent. As in Job's vision, when "the morning stars sang together," they are present at the moment of **spiritual genesis**, bearing witness to the Self's emergence from divine unity. They are also the **inner vibrations of conscience**, beauty, devotion, and vision—those stirrings within that remind the soul of its celestial origin.

As spiritual agents of Indra, they proclaim divine truth within the human heart. Their harmonious melodies help awaken the inner senses so that the thousand eyes of Indra—the faculties of divine perception—may open. They urge the soul upward, inspiring it to reclaim its light from the lower world and re-establish its consciousness in the spiritual domain.

Therefore, the Singers symbolize the **call of the Spirit within**—a symphony of divine energies reminding the soul that its true home is not among the cacophony of the lower nature ("people") but in the sublime stillness of truth, love, and divine sight.

The Descent of Purity and Truth from the Higher Planes

The sacred image of **two streams of water falling from heaven** at the moment of the Buddha's birth is not merely poetic—it is deeply metaphysical. These two streams are symbols of the **dual outpouring** of **Truth** and **Purity** flowing from the **atma-buddhi planes**—the highest spheres of spiritual consciousness—down into the soul's field of development. They descend not just to cleanse, but to **anoint**, to prepare the soul as a living vessel for divine realization.

In this image, **Indra**—the divine presence watching over this descent—is the **agent of spiritual deliverance**, holding the authority to release these heavenly waters. As the "thousand-eyed" principle of Divine Will, he governs the moment when the **spiritual rays of heaven pour down** upon the purified soul to awaken remembrance of its true origin.

The waters fall upon the head, the seat of intellect and identity. This represents the **baptism of the mind**—where thought is no longer merely functional but illuminated. The higher mind is not just informed; it is **transformed**. These waters wash away the residues of illusion and ego, allowing the crown (sahasrāra chakra) to become a **conduit of divine perception**—the full flowering of Indra's thousand eyes.

And just as the waters fall, they are accompanied by **Mandara flowers**, symbols of the soul's latent virtues. This means that the descent of Truth and Purity doesn't arrive alone—it **activates** the buried treasures within the soul, causing divine qualities to bloom. It is the **rain of Grace** that causes the garden of the Self to awaken from its long sleep.

When viewed metaphysically, **Water (Heaven)** is not only cleansing—it is **instruction**. It is the vibrational current of sacred knowledge, descending from the Upper Worlds and bathing the soul in clarity. It is also the element of emotional transmutation, turning the chaotic waters of desire into the crystal rivers of spiritual aspiration.

Thus, Indra, as sovereign over this descent, is the one who releases the heavenly waters **when the soul is ready**. He does not withhold them from the unworthy; he waits until the inner temple is built. Then, through purity of intention and spiritual readiness, the **light of heaven flows downward** and the Will of God is fulfilled in form.

Yama and Indra

The Causal Self and the Inner Throne of Judgment

Yama is widely known as the **Lord of Death**, but in metaphysical language, death is not the end—it is **transformation**, the passage from one state of being into another. In this deeper context, **Yama represents the Causal Self**, the perfected personality, the soul's **inner judge and ruler**, seated within the **higher mental plane**—the place of karmic synthesis, spiritual maturity, and evolutionary direction.

In the soul's inner architecture, **Indra and Yama** operate as twin powers—**Will and Judgment**, **Ascension and Accountability**. While Indra is the unwavering force that pushes upward toward union with the Divine, **Yama is the one who ensures that every step taken is authentic**, grounded in truth and earned through experience.

Yama governs the seat of karma—not in punishment, but in **divine equilibrium**. He holds the scale by which the soul's readiness for higher planes is measured. He does not block the path to heaven—he verifies that the soul is aligned with it. Where Indra commands movement toward the Highest, Yama enforces the **inner criteria** for that movement: sincerity, refinement, and spiritual integration.

In the **Śatapatha Brāhmaṇa**, Yama is associated with the sacred household fire (Gārhapatya), symbolizing the internal flame that sustains the soul's journey through lifetimes. Indra, in contrast, is linked to the altar fire (Ahavanīya), the sacrificial fire that reaches upward, calling down the Divine. Thus, the soul contains both fires: the **fire of devotion** that reaches up and the **fire of responsibility** that burns within.

Yama, as the **silent doorkeeper within**, asks the soul to look inward—not just at what it seeks, but at what it has become. His presence ensures that the rise of Indra is **not false fire**—not ambition masquerading as devotion, nor desire cloaked in spiritual language—but **true divine Will**, established on the firm foundation of soul maturity.

Together, Indra and Yama form a **sacred polarity**: the Will to ascend and the Wisdom to ascend rightly. Their union in the soul signifies that the Self is no longer impulsive or fragmented, but whole, radiant, and balanced.

YAMA, KING — THE CAUSAL SELF

(LAYER 1: AHAVANĪYA)

Yama, symbol of the Causal Self, stands as the perfected personality—fully integrated with divine will and wisdom. In the layered symbolism of the Self, Yama corresponds to the householder's sacred fire, **Gārhapatya**, while **Indra** is likened to the **Ahavanīya fire**, the flame of offering. Together, these spiritual fires reveal the dual outpouring from the higher nature: Indra as the divine spark radiating from **atma-buddhi**, and Yama as the causal flame seated within the **higher mental plane**.

The **Ahavanīya** fire represents the buddhic current of divine offering—the spiritual energy of sacrifice that flows from the Soul's inner altar. Indra, as the essence of this fire, projects the Divine Will into manifestation. This allows Yama, the inner king, to become the stable vehicle of that light. Through this connection, the higher mind becomes active, forming a bridge between the Divine and the aspirant. Yama thus rules the inner temple where the sacred flame of consciousness is preserved, echoing the role of the **Ahavanīya** as the sacrificial fire of heaven.

YAMA, KING — THE CAUSAL SELF

(LAYER 2: BUDDHIC PLANE)

To understand Yama fully, one must ascend to the **buddhic plane**, the luminous realm of divine intuition, where truth, wisdom, and unity interpenetrate all experience. Here, the **buddhi** is the soul's awakened light—the silent knowing of the higher Self, beyond intellect and emotion. It is the pure fire of direct perception.

Within this plane, Yama is no longer merely the perfected personality but becomes the living center of **spiritual discernment**. He operates as the **inner ruler** who has mastered duality and now functions as the balancer of karmic forces within the soul. While Indra pours spiritual vitality into this realm, Yama organizes, structures, and governs that influx as **lawful will** within the higher mind.

The buddhic plane is where separation ends and the soul begins to experience itself not as fragmented, but as whole. Yama, having mastered the personal trials of death, desire, and ego, now stands as the embodiment of equilibrium between **atma** (Spirit) and **manas** (Mind). He becomes the flame of measured thought governed by wisdom.

Thus, on the buddhic plane, Yama is not a judge in the worldly sense but a sovereign in the soul's sanctuary, presiding over the right use of will, the purity of aspiration, and the higher laws that bridge consciousness toward liberation.

YAMA, KING — THE CAUSAL SELF

(LAYER 3: Causal-Self)

Within the sacred framework of the soul's evolution, the **Causal Self** is the **inner temple**—a structure woven not from matter, but from memory, wisdom, and eternal identity. It is not the personality, which flickers and fades, but the **permanent essence** formed through cycles of moral triumph, spiritual insight, and purified emotion.

Here, Yama signifies the **sovereign of memory and meaning**, the keeper of all soul experiences accumulated over lifetimes. The Causal Self, formed through the union of mind and emotion on a higher octave, crystallizes as the **immortal soul-vehicle**—a radiant chamber where **wisdom, truth, and love** are stored as archetypal patterns.

Yama, in this domain, is the **ruler of the higher mental plane**, wherein he communicates to the lower self through **inner memory, symbols, and ideal forms**. He plants divine impressions—spiritual concepts, cosmic order, and soul directives—into the mental field of the evolving being. These impressions appear as "shadow-images," guiding the lower personality toward the light of remembrance and the clarity of soul knowledge.

Where Indra flows as divine will and energy, **Yama structures and preserves** the sacred knowledge of Self across incarnations. As the **Lord of the Causal Body**, Yama is thus the high priest of the inner sanctuary, holding the blueprint of our becoming—ever reminding the soul of its divine origin and its ultimate return.

YAMA, KING — DEATH AS SPIRITUAL SOVEREIGN

(LAYER 4: Death, King)

In its deepest mystery, **Death is not the destroyer—but the revealer.** Yama, as **Death**, signifies not the obliteration of life, but the final perfection of the **personality** that has passed through all earthly tests, all incarnations of ignorance and desire, and now stands exalted.

Yama, the **Son of Vivasvat**, represents the aspect of the Self that has **conquered the lower nature** and united with the Causal Self. Death comes **not as a punishment**, but as a reward to the perfected personality—now stripped of all illusion, purified of attachment, and luminous with divine knowledge.

He is **king** not because he rules over mortality, but because he **reigns over the transition from the mortal to the immortal**. The one who has faced life's fires and emerged with wisdom, now stands at the gate of liberation. As **King of Death**, Yama is the gatekeeper of transformation, the initiator into higher realities, and the embodiment of **self-mastery**.

Within every soul lies a **Nachiketas**—the seeker, the learner, the one who is instructed by Death. In myth, Nachiketas sits at Yama's feet to receive the eternal teaching. Metaphysically, this symbolizes the soul learning from its **own higher self** after lifetimes of experience, growing wise through joy, pain, loss, and love. In this encounter, Death becomes not the end, but the **final teacher**—and Yama, the soul's **crowned instructor**.

YAMA, KING — THE HOUSEHOLDER'S FIRE WITHIN

(LAYER 5: Gārhapatya)

The **Gārhapatya fire** is not an outer flame—it is the **inner hearth**, the sacred fire lit in the soul's sanctuary, where life's rituals are made sacred and the divine presence is welcomed home. It is the fire that **never leaves the house**—for the "house" is the **causal body**, and the fire is the **light of conscious evolution**.

Yama, as the **embodiment of this Gārhapatya flame**, is the **stabilizing presence** of divine order in the higher mind. He is the perfected personality that maintains the continuity of soul consciousness across incarnations, ensuring that the **soul remains centered**, even as it pours itself into form again and again.

Just as the Gārhapatya fire is kindled and sustained daily in Vedic ritual, Yama signifies the **eternal inner fire** that must be kept alive through discipline, devotion, and the pursuit of spiritual understanding. It is here that **karma is purified**, where memory is transmuted into wisdom, and where the **eternal seed** of the Self is safeguarded.

This fire is the **womb of rebirth**, the sanctified chamber where past efforts are transformed into future capacity. When the soul returns from earthly journeys, it finds rest at the hearth of Yama, the Causal King, who sits in the throne-room of the higher mental body, surrounded by the sacred flames of experience, judgment, and renewal.

In this way, **Yama is not the end of life—but the guardian of continuity**, the fire-keeper of the eternal Self within the house of the soul.

YAMA, KING — SHADOW OF THE FLAME

(LAYER 6: Indra)

If **Indra** is the blazing force of divine power—the thunderous will of the Higher Self—then **Yama** is the **measured shadow**, the reflection of that flame housed within form. Together, they represent two complementary faces of the **atma-buddhi-manas triad**: Indra as the **outpouring will**, Yama as the **inner seat of order and law**.

In the Śatapatha Brāhmaṇa, it is declared:

"Indra is the Ahavanīya fire. Yama is the Gārhapatya."

This cryptic pairing reveals a metaphysical key. **Indra**, as Ahavanīya, is the offering fire—the energy of sacrifice, divine will, and aspiration that calls the soul upward. **Yama**, as Gārhapatya, is the inward flame—the soul's power to **receive, organize, and preserve** that energy through the processes of incarnation.

Thus, Yama is the **inner receptacle** of Indra's thunder. He does not strike with lightning; he **stores the divine charge** within the soul's subtle bodies and governs how it is released through lifetimes. Where Indra stirs revolution, Yama ensures **evolution**. One is cosmic initiation; the other is karmic integration.

Together, they form the two poles of **spiritual development**: aspiration and stabilization, outward motion and inward rooting. And only when both are aligned can the divine Self unfold in its totality.

Yama is thus **Indra's echo** within the soul—not a lesser form, but a **harmonic container**, ensuring that the Light does not burn out the vessel before it has become strong enough to hold it.

YAMA, KING — THE TEACHER OF IMMORTALITY

(LAYER 7: Nachiketas)

In the timeless dialogue between **Yama** and **Nachiketas** in the Katha Upanishad, the soul's inner journey is revealed as a sacred confrontation: the **seeker** meets the **keeper** of the mystery.

Nachiketas, the questioning soul, stands for that part of the Self which has awakened to the hollowness of material offerings, ritual, and tradition. He refuses surface answers. He desires **truth**—not in theory, but in essence. He seeks the meaning of **death**, and in doing so, confronts **Yama**, the one who governs it.

Yama here is not a god of endings—but the **initiator into the eternal**. He tests the soul. He offers comforts, distractions, and pleasures—but Nachiketas resists. This resistance signifies the soul's readiness to receive the true **teaching of the Self**. And it is only to such a soul—pure in desire, strong in spirit, and firm in focus—that Yama reveals the immortal flame within.

This teaching is not intellectual. It is **experiential memory** passed from the Causal Self (Yama) to the awakening personality. What Nachiketas learns is not new; it is the remembrance of the **soul's original nature**, buried beneath layers of form and forgetfulness.

Thus, Yama becomes the **inner teacher**, revealing the mystery that the Self is **not born, nor does it die**, and that behind all change lies an unchanging **eternal witness**. The king of death becomes the **voice of eternity** within us—whispering the truths that cannot be taught by any outer book or priest.

In this light, **Yama is the master of transmission**, and **Nachiketas the pupil of remembrance**—two aspects of one soul, engaged in the sacred dialogue of awakening.

YAMA, KING — THE ASCENDED PERSONALITY

(LAYER 8: Personality)

The **personality** is often misunderstood as the "self"—but it is only a **shadow** cast by the greater light. It is the **temporary garment** worn by the soul for a single incarnation—a bundle of impressions, instincts, habits, and experiences gathered from the world below.

Yet when it is **perfected**, the personality becomes something more—it becomes a **vessel worthy of eternity**.

Yama, as **the King of perfected personality**, is not the mortal mask, but the soul's ability to master that mask. He signifies the **point of transmutation** where the lower self ceases to crave, struggle, or possess—and instead surrenders, refines, and becomes translucent to the light of the Higher Self. He is what remains after death has stripped away all illusion.

The **Causal Self**, or immortal soul, is built through the **sacrifice of countless personalities**, each shaped by karma, tested by time, and redeemed through will. Yama governs this alchemy—he is the **keeper of memory**, the architect of lessons integrated, and the judge not by condemnation, but by clarity. What survives is not ego, but **essence**.

Yama is the **silent recorder** of soul progress, the one who inscribes every thought, emotion, and deed into the fabric of the higher mental body. In this way, the personality is **not discarded, but transfigured**. It is raised from servant to sovereign, from mask to mirror, from fleeting actor to eternal witness.

And so, Yama is both **Death and Resurrection**—the proof that what is born of the earth may become worthy of heaven, and that what is temporal may be clothed in the robes of the immortal.

YAMA, KING — THE KEEPER OF DIVINE LIFE

(LAYER 9: Soma-juice)

Soma is more than a drink—it is the **life-blood of the cosmos**, the **sap of the Tree of Life**, the **nectar of immortality**. Where others see death, the wise see Soma flowing—veiled, but never absent. Yama is the one who **guards that flow**, for only the perfected Self can drink of it in truth.

In ancient hymns it is said:

"The gods drank of Soma and became immortal; men will become so when they drink with Yama…"

Metaphysically, this means: **immortality is not granted, but earned**—through purification, self-mastery, and devotion to the highest. Yama is not merely the king of endings—he is the **initiator into eternity**, the one who reveals Soma **only to the soul that has died to the lower** and now lives in harmony with divine law.

This Soma is not liquid, but **love fused with wisdom**—it is the life that flows through the **buddhic plane**, the pulse that sustains the higher mind, the "wine" of spiritual joy that nourishes the Causal Self. It is the **subtle communion** between the divine and the realized soul.

Yama, seated at the threshold between worlds, is the **dispenser of Soma**—not to the unready, but to the matured soul who has remembered its true nature. This is why in the Upanishads, **Yama offers Nachiketas the fire, the teaching, and the Soma**—for he is the **keeper of all three**.

To partake of Soma under Yama's kingship is to be **reborn in consciousness**, to be freed from fear, and to walk as one who is no longer bound to time but aligned with the eternal.

In totality, **Yama is the inner ruler of transition and truth**, the perfected personality transfigured by wisdom, the Causal Self luminous with memory, and the soul's silent witness who sits at the gate of immortality. He is not the god of death—but the **guardian of continuity**, the **archivist of wisdom**, and the **high priest of resurrection** within the temple of Self.

Closing Reflection — The Thousand Eyes Within

Indra is not a god of thunder and sky alone—he is the ever-watchful flame of **Divine Will** within you. His thousand eyes are not scattered across the heavens—they are seeded in your own consciousness, waiting to awaken, one by one, as you rise through the inner planes of truth.

He is the one within who remembers when you forget, who holds fast when the lower self trembles, who sees the path when your mind is clouded. He is the Will that endures not because it dominates, but because it **devotes**. He does not conquer through violence—he ascends through fidelity to the Light.

And though the "people" within—those lower thoughts, desires, and habits—may scoff, drown him out, or even seem to erase him, Indra is never truly gone. He waits in the sanctum of your being, in silence, in fire, in unwavering love of the Highest.

He is not a distant deity. He is your **inner resolve to serve what is eternal**.

He is the voice in your soul that says:
"Keep rising. Even now. Especially now."

And when the time comes—when your heart has been made clean by devotion, when your vision is no longer turned outward but inward and upward—he opens the gates.

You do not approach the Hall of Perfection alone.
You arrive with Indra.

And when you pass through that final door, it is because the Doorkeeper within you has stepped aside—
And the Divine in you has returned home.

RAMA CHAPTER 5

THE CAUSAL SELF — THE ETERNAL MEMORY OF THE SOUL

The **Causal Self** is not a fleeting personality, nor even the thinking mind—it is the **eternal core of individual identity**, formed through countless incarnations and spiritual triumphs. It is the **architect of meaning**, the one who collects, distills, and preserves every insight, every trial, every virtue acquired across lifetimes, and stores them as sacred blueprints for future becoming.

Where the lower self forgets, the **Causal Self remembers**. It is the **inner library** of the soul—every word, every symbol, every sacrifice recorded not in books, but in consciousness itself. When the higher Self speaks to the lower, it is this memory that becomes revelation. The Causal Self is the source of **true ideals**, the seeder of divine images into the mind. These are not fantasies—they are soul-coded impressions of wisdom, love, and truth, woven into the fabric of the inner being.

It is not abstract. It has **form**—a radiant vehicle composed of higher mind and purified feeling, shaped by sacrifice, built of light. The Causal Self is the **divine intermediary** between the Higher Self and the incarnated personality, delivering truth across dimensions of consciousness. Its symbols are not dead metaphors but **living seeds**, capable of awakening the divine within.

To reach the Causal Self is to awaken to one's **true identity—not as ego, but as soul**. It is the perfected "I" that no longer identifies with conditions, roles, or fleeting thoughts, but stands luminous and calm, knowing all things pass, and yet all things are known.

It is the **seat of sovereignty**, the bridge to immortality, the throne upon which the soul sits when it has remembered who and what it is.

THE CAUSAL BODY — THE CHARIOT OF THE SOUL

The **Causal Body** is the **soul's eternal vehicle**, the subtle yet indestructible form through which the **Causal Self** travels across cycles of manifestation. It is not made of matter, nor of thought, but of **soul-light**—a body of refined substance, shaped by wisdom, and sustained by truth.

This vehicle, also known as the **karana sharira**, is not an illusion—it is **realer than the physical**, because it endures while all outer forms pass away. It is called "causal" because it holds the **causes of all future growth**—the stored impressions of divine thought, noble emotion, and virtuous action. These impressions are the **seeds of karma**, preserved like sacred scrolls to be unfolded in future incarnations.

The Causal Body is composed of **buddhi-manas**—the fusion of intuitive wisdom and higher reason. It resides on the **higher mental plane**, above the noise of personality and below the stillness of the monad. In it is found the full **pattern of the individual soul**—its divine signature, its purpose, and its destiny. It is here that the Divine Will (Atma) is translated into meaningful form.

Just as the physical body moves through space, and the astral body through emotion, so does the Causal Body move through the **spiritual aether**, across lifetimes and in-between incarnations. It is the soul's **chariot of memory**, and it is this that **re-enters life clothed in new forms**, bearing forward the unfinished work of the Spirit.

This body is the **ark of spiritual continuity**. It carries within it the sacred relics of past devotion, past illumination, past mastery. And it is through this form that the divine self manifests as **heroes, avatars, prophets, and gods**—for the Causal Body is the **field where light becomes form**, and where form becomes **the divine instrument**.

When the ancient texts speak of **chariots of fire**, or of gods descending in flying craft, the mystic knows this is not mere mythology—it is the movement of the **Causal Body through the heavens**, guided by will, propelled by wisdom, and lit by the flame of purpose.

MAHĀBHĀRATA — The War of the Logos and the Great Originator Within

The Mahābhārata, in its deepest metaphysical sense, is not merely an ancient saga of dynastic conflict or terrestrial kingdoms. It is the eternal drama of the Soul—the conflict of the Logos, the Higher Self, manifesting through the incarnate mind, against the gravitational pull of the desire-nature, symbolized in esoteric language as Pūru, the shadow-asura who resists the inner Sun.

The name Mahābhārata translates to the "Great Bharata," or more accurately, "the Great Bearer," for it is Bharata—that which bears, upholds, and sustains the universe. In its true form, this Bearer is not a man, but a principle—the Divine Logos, which is expressed in manifestation as **Pragāpati**, the Great Architect and archetype of creative fire. Bharata, as Pragāpati, is the first vibration of God-consciousness in the soul's long descent and return. He is the Light that pervades all, the sustaining flame that holds the subtle architecture of the universe in place.

This Light, likened to the **sun**, represents the undivided radiance of the Higher Self—the indwelling Logos of man. Just as the visible sun illumines the physical world, the inner sun illumines the causal and mental planes. But its radiance is obscured when the soul descends into embodiment and identifies with the lower aspects of self. It is here that the desire-nature—symbolized as Pūru—arises as the great antagonist.

Pūru, in this sacred myth, is not a man but a distortion of will, a force within the soul that claims sovereignty through attachment to pleasure, sensation, and temporal power. As an **Asura** (demon of the lower world), Pūru is not inherently evil but represents energy that has lost its center in Truth. His resistance is the very friction through which the Logos must demonstrate Its supreme nature. Thus, the **Mahābhārata** becomes the stage upon which the Logos wages its holy war—not for conquest, but for integration and transformation.

Into this battlefield comes **Agni**, the flame-born Self, the incarnate intelligence of Divine Fire. It is through Agni—who is the operative force of purification and inner transmutation—that the Logos overcomes the lower forces. In esoteric psychology, this is the awakening of the spiritual will, which must battle the entrenchments of ego, desire, and illusion in order to reclaim the throne of the soul.

The Mahābhārata, then, is not just a tale. It is a metaphysical manual encoded in myth. It teaches that the divine conflict within is not a tragedy but an alchemical necessity. The desire-nature must rise so that it may be met, transmuted, and reabsorbed into the Light. In this war, every battle is sacred; every defeat is a lesson; and every victory is an ascent toward the reconstitution of the Higher Self in its fullness.

To study the Mahābhārata is to behold the secret of **God-manifest**—for in every soul lies a Pragāpati awaiting expression, a sun awaiting revelation, and a Pūru awaiting transmutation.

Pragāpati — The Divine Architect and the Bearing Flame

In the sacred drama of the Mahābhārata, Pragāpati is not merely a god among gods—he is the **originating Logos**, the divine architect whose very being becomes the lattice of all existence. To say that the Mahābhārata is a tale of dynastic war is to mistake shadow for source; for in truth, it is the war of the **Archetypal Man**—the one who bears, upholds, and sustains the cosmos, and whose soul is fragmented across the battlefield of time.

The name Bharata, meaning "Bearer," is a direct echo of **Pragāpati**, who is described in the esoteric texts as the **Great Bearer**, the one who shines like the sun and overthrows Pūru, the Asura of desire. But before he could become the luminous Logos that radiates across planes, Pragāpati had to descend, to fall, to be **dismembered** in sacrifice. He offered his very essence as the **life-sap of creation**, spilling forth into the lower worlds where his divine members became scattered as faculties of existence.

This sacrifice is echoed in every soul. For each soul is a fragment of Pragāpati's divine being, cast down into the world of forms to re-enact the journey of return. When the Sata Brāhmaṇa speaks of Pragāpati becoming "relaxed," it speaks of the **loss of the divine memory**, the dissociation of the Higher Self from its own fullness. The gods "leave him," and the soul, now isolated, begins its pilgrimage through incarnation.

In this sense, the **Mahābhārata** is the very **story of Pragāpati's restoration**—through conflict, through fire, through self-overcoming. The Logos, having once become latent within the soul, now wages a holy war within it. The battle between the Pandavas and Kauravas is the symbolic combat between the **intact divine seed (Agni)** and the **scattered forces of the desire-nature (Pūru, the Rākṣhasas)**. The Self must gather its own dismembered parts—will, mind, aspiration, discernment—and **rebuild the Godhead** within.

The chariot with **seven wheels and six spokes** in the Praśna Upanishad is the soul's own vehicle of ascent. These wheels correspond to the **seven globes of the planetary chain**, the stages of consciousness, while the six spokes mirror the **forces of evolution and involution**. Pragāpati, placed in the lower half, signifies the divine force **imprisoned in matter**, but still rotating the wheels of evolution from within.

Thus, the Mahābhārata is not merely the conflict between good and evil—it is **the alchemical transmutation of dismemberment into reconstitution**, of sacrifice into glory. The divine fire that was once "offered up" becomes the flame of spiritual will that burns through ignorance. As Pragāpati was restored by the gods through Agni, so too must the soul **rebuild its higher nature** by invoking the Fire within.

The war of Mahābhārata, then, is not an external war—it is the return of Pragāpati, the hidden Lord of Light, seeking to make whole what has been sundered, and to crown the soul once again as **the Bearer of God-consciousness**.

Agni — The Flame-Born Self Who Restores the Logos

If Pragāpati is the Architect of Divine Order, then **Agni** is the fire by which that order is **restored in the soul**. In the cosmic play of the Mahābhārata, Agni is not a lesser deity but the **incarnate intelligence of the Higher Self**, the divine will that enters the field of battle with one purpose: purification through fire.

Agni is the **flame of the soul**—the luminous strand of divine consciousness that still burns in the depths of the incarnate being. When Pragāpati became "relaxed," fragmented into the world of multiplicity, it was Agni who said, "I will enter into him, when whole." This is the great esoteric secret of all initiatic fire traditions: the soul must first be scattered and darkened so that it might **long for the flame**, and in longing, **ignite it again** from within.

In the metaphysical psychology of the Mahābhārata, Agni is the **spiritual will**—the fiery essence that awakens amidst the soul's despair and begins to transmute the baser elements. The field of Kurukshetra is not merely a literal battlefield, but the **inner terrain of the human being** where Agni wages war on ignorance, inertia, and desire.

Agni is the radiant essence within—the fire that dissolves impurity and reveals truth. When the soul offers itself upon this inner altar, it becomes luminous—prosperous in the material realm, and blissful in the higher dimensions of being.

Here, the sacrificer is none other than the personality—the mortal self—who offers its ignorance into the flame of truth. Agni receives this offering and transforms it. In doing so, the personality is crowned with **wisdom on earth** and **bliss in the higher realms**.

Agni, in the Brāhmaṇas, is also described as being established in the **innermost soul of the gods**, making them immortal and unconquerable. So too must the aspirant—like Arjuna—establish the fire in the core of their being. Only then does the soul gain the **force to overcome the asuras**—the lower appetites and distortions of divine energy.

In this way, Agni is both the **Destroyer and the Revealer**. He burns away illusion, but also illuminates the hidden essence. He is the brother of the Fire-God, the first-born of the divine womb, the heir of Osiris—and just as Osiris was torn and reconstituted, so too does Agni restore what was broken in Pragāpati.

Thus, in the Mahābhārata, Agni is not a background deity. He is the secret engine of transformation. He is **the inner Christ**, **the solar will**, **the divine flame** that cannot be extinguished by the tides of war or shadow. He purifies, illumines, and reclaims the soul's rightful throne—not through brute force, but through the luminous insistence of truth.

And so, **Agni is the returning Self**—the one who restores Pragāpati's broken body and reignites the Light that was momentarily lost. He is the flame of the

Mahābhārata, the sacred fire within the chariot of the soul, blazing through Kurukshetra to awaken God within man.

BHARATA — THE MORAL REGENT AWAITING THE RETURN OF THE LOGOS

In the grand symbolism of the Mahābhārata, **Bharata** is far more than a king or ancestral namesake. He is the **embodiment of the soul's moral conscience**, the one who holds the inner kingdom in balance until the **Higher Self**—the true King, the Logos—returns to claim it. He is the **Vice-King of Spirit**, entrusted with the guardianship of divine law in the absence of the blazing fire of Agni fully awakened.

The name Bharata itself means "Bearer"—and herein lies the key. What does he bear? Not only a kingdom, but the **burden and blessing of dharma**, the sacred order of the soul. In this role, Bharata mirrors a stage in spiritual evolution: that **intermediate condition** when the soul has awakened to higher truths, but the full fire of divine Selfhood has not yet descended.

Bharata assumes guardianship of the kingdom not for himself, but as a sacred trust. In reverence to the Higher Self symbolized by Rāma, he lifts the divine footprints—his shoes—to his head, placing duty beneath spirit, and acknowledging that true kingship belongs to the soul's inner flame.

The symbol is profound: **the shoes of Rāma** represent the **path already walked by the Higher Self**, the footprints of Spirit imprinted in the soul. Bharata places these on his head, signifying the **supremacy of spiritual authority over moral governance**. The moral nature recognizes it is not the end, but a means—a custodian preparing the soul for the divine return.

In this way, Bharata is the **righteous aspect of the incarnate soul** that maintains integrity, discipline, and sacred law in a world still under the influence of the lower nature. He does not claim the throne for himself—he waits, watches, and acts only in reverence to the **will of the Ideal**, which he knows must one day return in glory.

In the metaphysical conflict of the Mahābhārata, Bharata represents the **inner dharma-keeper**—the part of us that preserves order amidst chaos, that invokes divine remembrance in the absence of direct spiritual fire. This is the phase of the soul where **duty precedes devotion**, and **moral obedience** paves the path for **spiritual sovereignty**.

It is not by coincidence that Bharata belongs to the lineage of Pragāpati. He carries within him the **latent signature of the Great Architect**, and though he rules only in waiting, he bears the same divine DNA as the One he awaits.

So when we speak of the Mahābhārata as the war of the Logos, Bharata is not merely an ancestor but a **symbol of inner stability**, a **living altar** upon which the fire of Agni will soon descend. His reign is temporary, but his loyalty is eternal. He reminds us that **there is a part of the soul that always remembers God**, even when the fire has dimmed and the divine Self seems far away.

In the long night of the soul, Bharata watches the horizon for the return of the King.

Conflict — The Duality That Awakens the God Within

In the metaphysical blueprint of the Mahābhārata, **conflict is not the enemy**. It is the **hidden catalyst**— the churning force that compels the soul to rise above division and become whole. Without opposition, there would be no awakening; without war, there would be no peace worth knowing.

The Mahābhārata is not a tale of war in the ordinary sense —it is the **cosmic metaphor of opposition within**. The tension between spirit and matter, soul and personality, light and shadow, is encoded in every character and clash. The soul, descending through the planes, becomes entangled in the illusions of separation. And yet, within the heat of that struggle, something divine is forged.

Conflict and Victory are not opposites—they are twin aspects of a sacred process. On one side rises the friction that awakens the soul; on the other, the illumination that follows. Victory is not conquest—it is union with the Divine born from the tension of becoming.

This dual aspect—the necessary tension—is the central axis of spiritual evolution. It is through **not knowing**, through **limitation**, and through **the pressure of opposition** that the soul is driven to seek something beyond the veil. The Logos, hidden in the soul as latent flame, uses the very experience of duality to stir its own remembrance.

The soul is not meant to see the full arc of its journey while it walks the path. If it did, the fire of striving would be extinguished. It is precisely the soul's partial vision—its sacred limitation—that gives meaning to its unfolding. By forgetting its divine origin, the soul becomes the very seeker through which Truth is reawakened. This veil is not a curse, but a gift—for only through contrast can it declare the Light.

This is the paradox of spiritual combat. The soul must engage in a **sacred struggle**, not to destroy the other, but to **realize itself through contrast**. Every adversary is a mirror, every battle a lesson in higher perception. Conflict is the great revealer. It shows the soul what it is not, so it may remember what it is.

In the Mahābhārata, this conflict is personified by Pūru—the desire-nature—and Agni, the flame of Spirit. Their clash is not a punishment but a process: a divine necessity that transmutes baser energies into gold. Each swing of the sword, each test of loyalty, is a blow to the false self and a step toward the eternal Self.

The battlefield of Kurukshetra becomes a **sacred forge**, where the soul's latent divinity is tempered through strife. But conflict alone is not enough. Only when the soul confronts it with **courage, clarity, and fire** does it become alchemical.

This is why **Victory** is not external triumph—it is the **union with God** that comes when the fire of truth burns through duality. The victorious one is not he who conquers others, but **he who reconciles the parts within himself**. The war ends not in domination, but in **integration**.

Thus, in the metaphysical Mahābhārata, **Conflict is the initiation**. It is the serpent that bites, and the ladder that ascends. The soul must descend into it, must feel it, must wrestle with its own chaos—until, like Arjuna before Kṛṣṇa, it drops the weapons of ignorance and receives the blazing revelation of Self.

Rākṣasas — The Desire-Mental Host That Obstructs the Flame

In the sacred war of the Mahābhārata, **Rākṣasas** do not simply represent external enemies or dark forces—they are the **personified projections of the untransmuted mind**, the unresolved passions, fears, and falsehoods that **war against the soul from within**. They are the children of the lower rajas—the passionate, restless, pleasure-seeking current in the subtle body—and their dominion is the mind saturated with craving.

"Those of the quality of rajas worship the celestial powers—the Yakshas and Rākṣhasas... cloud demons who withhold the rains."
— Bhagavad-Gītā, Ch. XVII

To understand the Rākṣhasas is to understand how the **desire-nature weaponizes thought**. These beings are not merely base instincts; they are **mentalized distortions**, false philosophies, seductive distractions, and impulses that **simulate the divine** while steering the soul away from its true flame. They are the mental host of Pūru—the Asura who resists the inner sun.

In the metaphysical economy of the Mahābhārata, these Rākṣhasas are the **subtle adversaries** who obstruct the descent of Agni and resist the restoration of Pragāpati. They withhold the "rain"—a symbol of spiritual nourishment—and create arid landscapes within the soul, where **the flame flickers and the path is obscured**.

Beneath the tale of noble warriors and southern adversaries lies a deeper current—a mythic encoding of the soul's eternal conflict between the powers of inner light and the seductions of fragmented desire. The Rākṣhasas are not barbarians of land, but distortions of mind that rise when the soul forgets its divine origin.

These "barbarous races" are not peoples—they are **inner states of rebellion** against the divine order. Just as Rāma must wage war to reclaim Sītā, the soul must confront these distorted thought-forms that have **kidnapped its sacred feminine**—the intuitive, receptive aspect of divine knowing. Sītā is the soul's deeper truth, and the Rākṣhasas are the forces that attempt to **sever her from the Logos**.

In the battlefield of Kurukshetra, the Rākṣhasas appear as the confusion of war—the misplaced loyalties, the egoic justifications, the clamor of opposing voices within the psyche. They are illusions clothed in belief. They come from within, and they can only be defeated from within.

And yet—here is the mystical key—they are not evil in essence. They are **misused power**, fragments of will and mind that have **lost alignment with Truth**. The Rākṣhasas are not destroyed by hatred but by transmutation. The Logos must reclaim them. They must be purified by Agni and reabsorbed into the divine economy of the soul.

Thus, the Mahābhārata teaches us that the soul must descend not just into outer conflict, but into **mental purification**. The true war is against false light—the deceptive voices that mimic wisdom but are born of separation. To conquer them is not to kill, but to awaken—to shine the sun of the Logos so brightly that all shadows lose their form.

When this final veil is pierced, and the Rākṣhasas no longer hold sway over the inner kingdom, the full descent of Pragāpati becomes possible. The divine fire floods the soul, and the war ends not in annihilation, but in the **return of divine order**.

THE MAHĀBHĀRATA — The Sacred War of Descent and Divine Return (Final Synthesis)

The Mahābhārata is more than epic—it is the living symbol of the soul's pilgrimage through creation. It does not merely recount the battles of kings, but unveils the **eternal war waged within each human being**, where the spark of the divine must pass through the veils of illusion to reclaim its throne.

At the origin of this war stands **Pragāpati**, the Great Bearer. He is not a god among gods, but the divine impulse at the heart of creation—the One who sustains, radiates, and sacrifices. His descent is not a fall, but a sacred offering. Fragmented across the planes of existence, his divine essence becomes the blueprint of every soul. What was whole is scattered; what was luminous becomes latent. Yet within this scattering lies the mystery: a **call to be made whole again**.

The fire that answers this call is **Agni**. Not a flame in the sky, but the **inner fire of awakened will**, the spiritual current that burns within the temple of the soul. Agni is the first to rise when the soul begins to remember. He is the sacred unrest, the divine dissatisfaction that compels the seeker forward. Through him, the soul becomes the sacrificer—offering up its illusions so that truth may rise. He does not destroy for the sake of vengeance, but purifies to restore divine order. In his flames, **ignorance dissolves**, and the scattered pieces of the Self begin to reunite.

Yet before the Logos can reign, there must be a guardian. **Bharata** steps forward as the soul's moral strength—the one who rules in reverence, not pride. He does not mistake himself for the flame, but **bows to it**, holding the inner kingdom in sacred preparation. He represents the phase in which the soul governs itself by principle, awaiting the day when love and wisdom will replace duty and law. In Bharata, the soul honors what is to come, even when the fire has not yet fully descended.

But this journey is not free of turmoil. The path to divine remembrance is marked by **conflict**—not because the soul is broken, but because it must be **forged**. Every moment of duality, every pressure of opposition, becomes the alchemical ground through which the Logos proves its essence. Conflict is not failure—it is **friction with purpose**, the sacred tension that awakens the desire to know, to remember, to return. Through struggle, the soul clarifies its allegiance—toward the light, not illusion.

And in the midst of this struggle rise the **Rākṣhasas**—not monsters of myth, but **the shadows of the soul's own mind**, distorted by attachment, fear, and craving. They are the unrefined forces that block the rain of divine nourishment, the clouded thoughts that mimic wisdom but reject the fire of real transformation. These adversaries are not to be hated, but transmuted. They represent parts of the self that have lost their center—and through the fire of Agni and the patience of Bharata, they too may be reclaimed.

Thus, the Mahābhārata is not a tale of ancient India—it is a tale of **every soul**. It is the **blueprint of divine**

reintegration, encoded in the language of myth, waiting to be read by the inner eye. Within its battles, we find our own. Within its heroes, we see our Higher Self. And in its victory, we glimpse not domination—but **divine reunion**.

The Logos returns.

The bearer is restored.

The fire is whole.

The Mental Plane — The World of Formed Thought and Celestial Pattern

The **Mental Plane** is the luminous middle-world of consciousness, the **bridge between Spirit and matter**, where **archetypal ideas descend into vibration and structure**. It is neither of earth nor entirely of the heavens—it is the creative threshold, the sacred echo chamber where divine will begins to **shape itself into form**.

This is not a metaphor—it is a metaphysical law. All things that come into being **pass through the mental plane**, for it is the **architectural field** through which Spirit enters embodiment. Here, unspoken truths, divine blueprints, and luminous patterns are **translated into symbolic geometry**, ready to descend through the astral and physical veils.

To understand the mental plane is to understand the soul's own creative engine. Every divine principle—be it justice, beauty, or purpose—first takes shape here, like a **subtle body of thought**, formed in luminous mental matter before being projected outward. It is here that **Logos becomes Law**, and idea becomes image.

But the mental plane is not pure in all directions. It is also the realm of **distortion**—where thought, descending through interference, may be fragmented or obstructed. In its upper currents, the mental plane reflects the **form of truth**, the sacred prototypes of all being. But in its lower strata, it is entangled with desire, memory, and illusion.

What descends as wholeness may arrive fragmented; what begins as divine intention may reach the physical world veiled in confusion.

This is why **mental clarity is spiritual responsibility**. The soul creates constantly—not just by action, but by thought. Every mental image, every inner structure, is a blueprint that seeks embodiment. And thus, the soul is not only a vessel—it is a **constructor of realities**, a force that coalesces matter around its dominant thought-forms.

The **mental plane is not abstract**. It is the **subtle architecture of the world**. Everything we see has passed through it, shaped by thought-forms, desires, ideals, and archetypes. From a seed to a system, from a star to a soul—all things are born of **mental patterns in vibration**.

And yet, it is not the final plane. It is a **liminal space**, where the soul either ascends toward spirit or descends into fragmentation. Those who dwell only in the mind, divorced from the higher Self, become trapped in infinite reflections—clever, but disembodied; knowing, but not becoming. For the mind without spirit becomes a mirror with no light.

But for the one who awakens the fire within, the mental plane becomes a sacred tool—an altar of thought upon which divine ideas are crystallized into reality. In this way, the mental plane is the **womb of manifestation**—not because it holds power itself, but because it receives power from above and channels it downward with precision.

To master the mental plane is not to conquer thought—it is to **consecrate it**. It is to become the priest of one's own inner temple, offering only those thoughts that serve the divine pattern. For in this plane, thought is fire, and the soul is the forge.

Mental Plane and the Builders of the Universe: The Architects of Celestial Thought

The **Mental Plane**, as the central field of divine translation, is not an empty realm—it is **populated and structured** by the **first-born intelligences**: the Builders of the Universe. These are not metaphorical figures—they are conscious agents of form, emanating from the Godhead to initiate the architecture of the inner worlds. In the metaphysical order, they are the **Archangels, Devas, and primordial Messengers** who descend first, **not to govern, but to design**.

Just as the **Mental Plane** receives the pure idea and shapes it into image, so do these **Builders** receive the Divine Will and translate it into geometry, vibration, and law. They are not the end product of evolution, but the **initial carriers of divine structure**, emerging on the **highest subplanes of the mental world**, shaping the descent of thought before it enters the astral and physical.

Their task is to create the **invisible scaffolding of reality**—not by effort, but by **emanation**. Their very being is the patterning force. These Builders are the

organizing intelligences of the mental field; they are **the reason why thought has form**. Where there is sacred proportion, archetype, rhythm, or higher logic, the presence of these Builders can be sensed. They **do not speak—they structure**. They impress.

And they do not operate from a distance. The human soul, as it evolves, begins to awaken this same **Builder consciousness** within itself. When the mind becomes still, clear, and aligned, it becomes a **microcosmic builder**—a reflector of the celestial architect. This is why mental discipline and spiritual thought are holy: they allow the soul to **participate in the same work as the Archangels**—to shape reality through divine Idea.

Thus, the **Mental Plane is the Builder's Temple**. Within it, **prototypes are crystallized**, **monads are named**, and **thought becomes architecture**. From here, the Builders send forth their emanations, which descend as form—first subtle, then material.

But this also demands reverence. For to pollute the mental plane with chaotic, disordered thought is to interfere with the sacred blueprint. Each soul, when thinking, is either participating with the Builders or erecting shadows beside them.

Pragāpati and the Builders — The Dismembered Logos as Cosmic Substance:

The Sacrificed Self as the Blueprint of Creation

If the **Builders of the Universe** are the architects, then **Pragāpati (relaxed)** is the **living blueprint**, the divine substance offered to them as the very **material of creation**.

In esoteric doctrine, Pragāpati is not just the divine being who creates—he is the one who **offers himself up to become the cosmos**. His "relaxation" is not exhaustion; it is **sacrificial release**. The life-force, once held in concentrated form, is poured out, diffused into the mental, astral, and physical worlds as raw essence. This is **the sacred dismemberment**—the fragmentation of the Archetypal Man into the elements of structure, vibration, and time.

To the Builders, this sacrificed Logos becomes the **garment of God**—the layered sheath through which divine will can be shaped into visible reality. The Builders do not invent form from nothing. They use the **fallen light of Pragāpati**—his limbs, his life-sap, his spiritual memory—as the clay from which to mold the invisible worlds.

Thus, every thought-form birthed on the mental plane is **encoded with the memory of the Whole**. Every mental structure is **a fragment of the Great Self**—a remnant of that primordial Being who gave his fullness to become the cosmos. This is why the soul, as it evolves, feels the call to rebuild—it is echoing the original sacrifice, attempting to gather the scattered pieces of its own divine ancestry.

Pragāpati, then, is not separate from the Builders. He is **within the structure they create**. He is the **sacred pattern buried in the mental plane**, waiting to be reassembled by the awakened mind. As the soul ascends and begins to build consciously, it is not only constructing —it is **remembering**, **gathering**, **resurrecting**.

In this light, the Builders are not simply engineers. They are **priests of the sacrificed Logos**, shaping the cosmos as a temple to the One who gave Himself to become it. And the mental plane is the altar upon which this silent ritual eternally unfolds.

Rama Chapter 6

The Soul's Ascent in the Chariot of Light: Rama Prepares to Return to Ayodhya

(Based on Yuddha Kāṇḍa, Chapter 121)

After a restful night, Rama, the vanquisher of foes, awoke refreshed. Vibhishana, approaching him with joined palms, addressed him respectfully:

"Lord Rama, these women, adorned with lotus-like eyes and skilled in the art of decoration, have brought bathing essentials—garments, ornaments, sandalwood paste, and exquisite garlands. They are prepared to assist you in your ceremonial bath."

Upon hearing Vibhishana's offer, Rama responded:

"Invite Sugriva and the other monkey chiefs to partake in this bathing ritual. However, my heart longs for Bharata, the virtuous prince who has been enduring hardships on my behalf. Until I reunite with him, such luxuries do not appeal to me."

"Our immediate concern should be determining how to return swiftly to Ayodhya. The journey is arduous, and time is of the essence."

Vibhishana replied:

"Great prince, I can ensure your arrival in Ayodhya within a day. The celestial aerial car, Pushpaka—once belonging to my brother Kubera but seized by Ravana—is at your disposal. This magnificent vehicle moves according to one's will and shines brilliantly like the sun. It stands ready to transport you effortlessly to your kingdom."

"O Rama, if you deem me worthy of your kindness and hold any affection for me, please consider staying in Lanka a while longer. Allow me the honor of hosting you, Lakshmana, and Sita, offering you the hospitality that has been lovingly prepared. I make this request not as a command, but as a humble servant devoted to your service."

Rama, acknowledging Vibhishana's sentiments, replied:

"Your counsel, unwavering dedication, and friendship have deeply honored me. However, my heart is set on reuniting with Bharata, who once journeyed to Chitrakuta to persuade me to return, a request I could not fulfill then. My mother Kausalya, Sumitra, Kaikeyi, my friend Guha, the citizens of Ayodhya, and the surrounding populace—all await my return."

"Kind Vibhishana, please permit me to depart. Your hospitality is cherished, but my yearning to see my loved ones compels me to leave without delay."

Understanding Rama's earnest desire, Vibhishana promptly summoned the Pushpaka Vimana. This resplendent aerial car, radiant as the sun, was adorned with golden features, platforms of cat's-eye gems, and structures that gleamed like silver. Decorated with white flags and golden lotuses, it boasted stately mansions, networks of melodious tiny bells, and crystal-inlaid pavements. Furnished with exquisite seats upholstered in precious coverings, it stood as a testament to divine craftsmanship.

Informing Rama of the Pushpaka's readiness, Vibhishana stood aside. Rama, along with Lakshmana, marveled at the celestial vehicle's grandeur, resembling a towering mountain, capable of traveling anywhere at the owner's behest.

Metaphysical Interpretations

In this passage, each character and element symbolizes profound aspects of the spiritual journey:

- **Rama** represents the **Higher Self** or **Divine Consciousness**, the ultimate realization of one's spiritual essence.

- **Vibhishana** embodies the **discerning intellect** that, having turned away from the dominance of ego and desire (Ravana), now aligns with divine will, facilitating the soul's return to its true abode.

- **Sugriva and the monkey chiefs** symbolize the **primal energies and instincts** that, once chaotic, have been transformed into allies through disciplined spiritual practice.

- **Bharata** signifies the **moral and ethical foundation** within, the unwavering virtue that remains steadfast even when the conscious self is diverted from its path.

- **The women with lotus-like eyes** represent the **refined faculties of intuition and emotion**, offering their beauty and grace to honor the awakened Self.

- **Pushpaka Vimana**, the celestial aerial car, denotes the **vehicle of higher consciousness** or the **light body**, enabling transcendent movement beyond physical limitations, guided solely by the will of the enlightened self.

- **Ayodhya** symbolizes the **state of inner harmony and spiritual fulfillment**, the ultimate destination where the Higher Self reunites with its moral core and divine companions.

Rama's refusal of indulgent rituals until reuniting with Bharata illustrates the enlightened being's prioritization of inner virtue over external adornments. The swift journey via Pushpaka signifies the accelerated ascent to higher states of consciousness once alignment with divine will is achieved.

This narrative encapsulates the soul's triumphant return from the realm of ego and desire (Lanka) to its rightful place of inner peace and divine unity (Ayodhya), guided by discernment, supported by transformed instincts, and transported by the vehicle of elevated awareness.

Metaphysical retelling: The Soul's Ascent in the Chariot of Light

After the conquest of the lower nature—when the inner fire had defeated the ten-headed distortion of desire and illusion (Rāvaṇa)—the purified intellect (Vibhīṣaṇa), once aligned with darkness but now turned fully toward the Spirit, approached the Flame of the Higher Self (Rāma), who had arisen renewed after the battle. With devotion in his being, the purified intellect (Vibhīṣaṇa) spoke:

"O Radiance of the Soul (Rāma), vessels of beauty and intuition stand ready. The refined aspects of nature—the lotus-eyed faculties of subtle emotion and inner clarity (the women with lotus-like eyes)—arrive bearing sacred tools of purification: garments of new thought, ornaments of perfected virtue, fragrant pastes of devotion, and garlands woven from spiritual insight. Let them anoint you—for you are now Sovereign over the inner kingdom."

But the Flame of the Higher Self (Rāma) turned gently and said:

"Invite the primal energies of devotion and strength (Sugrīva and the monkeys)—those wild but loyal impulses purified through service—to this rite. Yet know this: my return to the divine center of will (Bharata), that noble essence who renounced the world's pleasures for the soul's rightful order, must come before any adornment. The moral essence within me—the youth of truth, unshaken though delicate (Bharata)—has endured exile during my descent into matter. Until I am reunited with this essence, no ritual, no ornament, no jewel brings satisfaction."

"And how shall we cross the veils and landscapes of time to reach the throne of Truth (Ayodhyā)? This path back to the divine order is long, unclear."

To this, the purified intellect (Vibhīṣaṇa) answered:

"O Sovereign Flame (Rāma), I will carry you beyond limitation. The celestial vehicle (Puṣpaka vimāna)—once belonging to Divine Abundance (Kubera), stolen long ago by the lower desire-nature (Rāvaṇa)—is now reclaimed. This chariot, born of divine architecture (Vishvakarma), responds not to reins but to will. Shining like the spiritual sun, it moves by thought, glides by intention, and stands ready at your command."

"If I have won your trust, if virtue binds us in friendship, grant me the grace to serve you longer. Let the remaining forces of the psyche—your companions in this inner war (the monkey army)—receive the hospitality of devotion. Let all parts of the soul taste rest before the great return. I speak not as one who commands, but as one who serves Light."

The Flame of the Self (Rāma), honored deeply, spoke amidst the awakened energies—some once demonic impulses (rākṣasas), now tamed, and others the beast-forces (monkeys) transfigured by loyalty:

"You have honored me more by your understanding than by any gift. But know this: my entire being races toward reunion with the moral conscience (Bharata)—who once knelt in surrender at the mountain of decision (Mount Chitrakūṭa), begging my return. My task is done. My fire no longer belongs here among shadows. The thread of destiny calls me to the throne of truth (Ayodhyā)."

He recalled the moral essence (Bharata) who knelt in supplication... the inner mother-principles of love (Kausalyā), wisdom (Sumitrā), and karma (Kaikeyī) who watched from afar... the friend of instinctual purity (Guha) who waited by the river of memory... and the collective soul-energies of the entire spiritual body (citizens and countrymen) longing for restoration.

"Grant me departure," said the Flame (Rāma). "You have given me much—but now I must return."

Then the purified intellect (Vibhīṣaṇa) summoned forth the celestial vehicle—the Chariot of Light (Puṣpaka vimāna), born of divine thought:

It shone like sacred architecture, gilded with the symbols of inner fire and adorned with jewels of vision (gold and cat's-eye gems). Its pillars were of golden lotus—symbols of awakened potential. Its canopy bore flags of divine breath (white banners), and its foundations sang with the resonance of truth (tiny bells). Bells of recognition whispered along its edges, and its form shimmered like Mount Meru—the axis of spiritual consciousness. Crafted by the Architect of the Gods (Vishvakarma), its corridors were paved with crystallized insight and clothed in coverings woven from remembrance (pearls, crystal, and sacred fabric).

Before this celestial chariot stood the Flame of the Self (Rāma)—accompanied by the Will (Lakṣmaṇa) and the Intuition (Sītā), ascending not into the sky, but into the realm beyond distortion, toward the Eternal Seat of Divine Governance—the throne of the true "I Am" (Ayodhyā).

Hanuman's Return & Rāma's Praise (The Soul Receives the Truth-Bearing Messenger)

(Source: chapter 1, Yuddha kanda)

Rama Appreciates Hanuman:

After Hanuman returned from his mission to Lanka, he approached Rama and recounted his journey, detailing how he had discovered Sita in the Ashoka grove, conveyed Rama's message to her, and observed the fortifications of Lanka. Rama listened intently, his heart swelling with gratitude and admiration. Overcome with emotion, Rama embraced Hanuman warmly and said, "Hanuman, the task you have accomplished is extraordinary and beyond the capabilities of anyone else. By finding Sita and bringing back vital information, you have safeguarded our lineage and given me renewed hope." Despite his profound appreciation, Rama felt a pang of sorrow, realizing he had no gift worthy of Hanuman's unparalleled service. He expressed, "In these circumstances, all I can offer you is my heartfelt embrace as a token of my gratitude." Turning his thoughts to the impending challenge, Rama contemplated, "Now, we must devise a strategy to cross the vast ocean with our army to rescue Sita."

Metaphysical Retelling: The Higher Self Acknowledges Devoted Mind

After the devoted mind, unwavering in its purpose (Hanuman), returned from its journey into the realm of ego and illusion (Lanka), it approached the Higher Self

(Rama) and recounted its quest. The devoted mind detailed how it had located the soul's pure essence (Sita) within the grove of inner tranquility (Ashoka grove), communicated the Higher Self's intention, and assessed the strongholds of the ego. The Higher Self listened deeply, its being swelling with gratitude and admiration. Overcome with profound connection, the Higher Self embraced the devoted mind and spoke: "O embodiment of unwavering dedication (Hanuman), the mission you have fulfilled is beyond ordinary capacity. By rediscovering the soul's pure essence (Sita) and bringing back this vital insight, you have preserved the integrity of our spiritual lineage and rekindled my hope." Despite this deep appreciation, the Higher Self felt a moment of sorrow, realizing that no material offering could equate to the devoted mind's unparalleled service. It expressed, "In this present state, all I can offer is the embrace of my true self as a symbol of my boundless gratitude." Turning attention to the next challenge, the Higher Self contemplated, "Now, we must determine how to transcend the vast sea of worldly illusion to reunite with the soul's pure essence (Sita)."

Ravana Consults His Ministers: Yuddha Kāṇḍa (Book of War), Rāmāyaṇa

(Source: Approximate Chapter Number - Yuddha Kāṇḍa, Sarga 17–19)

In the secret hall of Lanka, where pillars shone with infernal opulence and shadows moved with pride, the ruler of the Rakshasas, Ravana, seated upon a throne of obsidian, summoned his ministers after a sleepless night. The king of ten heads, burdened with thoughts of war and wounded pride, was cloaked in dark armor reflecting both glory and fear.

He turned toward his counselors and said, "Victory has eluded us. My armies have faltered. That prince of Dharma, Rama, stands undefeated, and our strongest warriors have fallen. What remains to be done? Shall we gather what strength is left and strike once more, or seek another path?"

The ministers—creatures of cunning and illusion, loyal to Ravana's will—rose one by one. Each spoke in favor of war, inflamed by vengeance and ego. "Why retreat? You are the lord of Lanka! The heavens themselves once trembled at your roar. Let no fear shake you now. We shall gather the remaining Rakshasas and wage one final assault."

One voice stood apart. Vibhishana, the brother of Ravana, calm and discerning, stepped forward with folded palms. "Brother, let reason prevail. Your strength is great, but not greater than destiny. This Rama, prince of Dharma, is not an ordinary being. He fights not for conquest, but for truth. His cause is just. Let us seek peace, lest the entire kingdom fall in ruin."

Ravana, inflamed with pride and fury, thundered back, "You dare counsel surrender? My power forged this kingdom! I will not bow! Leave, if your heart no longer beats for Lanka."

Vibhishana, saddened but resolute, turned from the court and departed, choosing truth over blood-ties.

METAPHYSICAL RETELLING: THE COUNCIL OF THE DESIRE-MIND (RAVANA CONSULTS HIS MINISTERS)

Within the stronghold of the lower self, where the architecture of ego had raised a kingdom atop illusion, the desire-mind (Ravana) brooded restlessly. Though robed in power, his many aspects of delusion (ten heads) churned in conflict. The shadows that once obeyed now whispered of uncertainty, and so he summoned his inner faculties—those loyal voices of justification, pride, and stubborn force.

"O agents of my will," the desire-mind (Ravana) declared, "the Light of the Self (Rama) draws near. My creations tremble before it. What counsel shall you offer, now that my fortress is shaken?"

The voices of illusion rose—the inner ministers of the astral self, personified energies bound to the flesh and indulgence. "Strike harder!" they cried. "We are the rulers of perception, the kings of passion and indulgence. The Self cannot overthrow us. Let us mount one final resistance."

Then entered scientific discrimination (Vibhishana)—the mind awakened by knowledge and clarity, once serving the desire-nature but now aligned with higher discernment. With joined palms, this voice of clarity spoke:

"O fallen majesty, your era ends. The Incarnate Self (Rama) does not wage war for dominance but to restore harmony. You are no longer the axis of power—truth has arrived. If you persist in illusion, all your works will burn. Surrender now to the Will of the Higher Self."

But the desire-mind (Ravana), intoxicated with self-image and past glory, roared back, "I will never surrender! My kingdom was forged by might and shall fall by none!"

And so, scientific discernment (Vibhishana) departed the palace of delusion. He turned from the intoxicating glow of the lower world, aligning with the Soul's cause, choosing truth over attachment.

Vibhishana Seeks Refuge with Rama

Yuddha Kanda – Valmiki Ramayana, Book of War
Theme: Integration of the Scientific Mind into the Higher Self's Journey
Source: Yuddha Kanda, Chapter 16 (also found in Valmiki Ramayana translations)

After witnessing the cruelty of his brother Rāvana and realizing the futility of his arrogance, Vibhīṣaṇa, the righteous brother of the demon king, resolved to abandon Laṅkā and seek shelter with Rāma. Accompanied by four of his companions, he rose into the sky and crossed the ocean to reach the encampment of the vanaras.

Seeing a figure approaching from the sky, the monkey warriors were alarmed and reported it to Sugrīva. Hanumān, however, recognized Vibhīṣaṇa and advised Sugrīva not to judge him by his origin alone. Sugrīva, still cautious, brought the matter to Rāma.

When informed, Rāma listened intently and said with compassion:
"He who seeks refuge, even if he were my enemy, must not be turned away. What to speak of one who comes with folded hands, speaking the truth. Even if Rāvana himself were to come seeking protection, I would offer it without hesitation. Bring Vibhīṣaṇa to me."

Thus, Vibhīṣaṇa was brought before Rāma, bowed humbly, and declared his renunciation of Rāvaṇa's kingdom. Rāma welcomed him with honor and embraced him as a brother. He assured Vibhīṣaṇa that he would be installed as the rightful king of Laṅkā once Rāvaṇa was defeated.

Metaphysical Retelling: The Scientific Mind Seeks the Flame of the Self

After the crumbling of false allegiance and the exposure of corrupted desire, the scientific mind (Vibhīṣaṇa)—long aligned with the domain of distorted appetites (Rāvaṇa)—became disillusioned. Realizing the deception of clinging to the lower nature (Laṅkā), he ascended from its vibration and crossed the sea of duality to approach the Sovereign Flame of the Self (Rāma).

He was accompanied by four aspects of rational discernment—powers of reasoning refined by inner clarity—and his presence in the sky startled the instinctual faculties (vanaras), who reported the phenomenon to the primal intelligence of devotion (Hanumān) and the leader of directed will (Sugrīva).

Though the impulsive self (Sugrīva) hesitated, the awakened intellect (Hanumān) offered counsel: "Judge not by origin, but by direction. The mind that turns toward Light, though born from darkness, deserves reception."

When brought before the Incarnate Flame (Rāma), the Higher Self spoke:
"Any who turns from illusion and seeks Truth, I accept without condition. Even if the desire-mind (Rāvaṇa) himself were to renounce falsehood, I would shelter him."

And so, the scientific mind (Vibhīṣaṇa) approached with reverence and renounced the astral throne. The Flame of the Self embraced him, not as a former foe, but as an ally of evolution.

"I make you ruler of the once-shadowed domain," said the Flame.
"For it is the mind illumined by virtue that must govern the desire-realm—not tyranny, but truth shall reign."

Rama Marches Toward Lanka

Source: Yuddha Kāṇḍa, chapter 27 – "Rama Advances to Lanka"

Having made final preparations, the noble prince **Rama**, driven by dharma and purpose, gathered his vast army of **Vanaras** and **Rakshasas** loyal to the cause. **Sugreeva**, king of the forest-dwellers, stood at his side, directing units of warriors with immense strength and agility. **Hanuman**, filled with unwavering devotion, remained ever near, his gaze fixed on the horizon beyond the ocean.

The ocean itself lay stretched before them—vast, unending—a daunting expanse separating their camp from **Lanka**, the fortress of the formidable **Ravana**.

Rama, resolute, gazed toward the southern shores. "We shall not turn back. Let the bridge be built. Let the waters be crossed. The time of action has arrived."

In obedience to this divine command, **Nala**, son of the celestial builder, led the **Vanaras** in constructing the bridge. Trees were felled, rocks were rolled, and mighty mountains were placed into the depths of the sea. The creatures of the wild toiled as one, invoking the power of unity and devotion.

After days of effort, the bridge stretched across the ocean, connecting earth to **Lanka's** shores. With arms poised and eyes aflame with spiritual intensity, **Rama** led the march across the ocean, signaling the great invasion that would shake the foundations of illusion itself.

Metaphysical Retelling – The Descent into Desire

The Bridge Across the Abyss of Illusion

The **Higher Self (Rama)**, whose will had been forged in fire, stood upon the edge of the subconscious sea—the veil that separates the awakened spirit from the entanglement of base desire. Around him gathered the **mental energies shaped by instinct and service (Vanaras)** and the once-opposing but now loyal **transformed passions (Rakshasas)**.

At his right hand stood the **discipline of natural loyalty and strength (Sugreeva)**. To his left, the **Intellect awakened by the breath of Spirit (Hanuman)**, unwavering in his service, awaited the next sacred task.

Before them surged the ocean—the **great subconscious**, the **astral realm**, filled with the tides of karmic memory, emotional residue, and ancient attachments. It was not just water—it was **the abyss of illusion**, the psychic boundary every soul must cross on its path to liberation.

The **Divine Flame (Rama)** spoke:
"We shall not remain in partial awakening. The bridge must be formed. Let Thought and Will span the gap. Let the path to the innermost fortress of distortion be revealed."

He summoned **Constructive Intelligence (Nala)**—that divine faculty born of the **Architect of the Cosmos (Vishvakarma)**—to lead the task. Stones of sacred thought, trees of refined passion, and mountains of disciplined will were cast into the ocean of the subconscious, each becoming a step toward divine embodiment.

The army of faculties moved as one. Each mind-cell, each emotion, each latent power took its place in constructing the **Path of Light over the Sea of Samsara**.

And when it was complete, the **Flame of the Self (Rama)** strode forward—not into war, but into **integration**.

Behind him followed the **psycho-spiritual forces of the soul**, marching not with violence, but with the intent to **liberate the soul trapped within the fortress of illusion (Lanka)** and to confront the **Desire-Mind (Ravana)** at its throne.

Ravana Reacts to the March of Rama's Army

(Source: Chapter 28, Book of War, Yuddha Kanda)

Ravana, the sovereign of Lanka, sat upon his throne in the council hall, surrounded by his ministers. The sounds of war drums and the march of Rama's advancing army, composed of Vanaras led by Sugreeva and Hanuman, echoed through the air. His face bore both fury and unease. The great demon-king turned to his advisors and demanded:

"What is this thunder that shakes Lanka's earth? Who dares bring such force against my command?"

One of his counselors responded, "O mighty Ravana, it is Rama, the prince of Ayodhya, who has crossed the ocean by constructing a great bridge. He comes with Sugreeva, the monkey-king, and Hanuman, the son of the wind, along with an army that covers the land like ants upon sugarcane."

Another minister, full of arrogance, sneered: "These Vanaras are mere beasts. Let us not tremble before creatures that swing from trees. With your power, O Ravana, they shall be turned to dust."

Yet another spoke with more caution: "Do not underestimate Rama. He has defeated countless warriors, including Khara and Dushana. Even Vali, the mightiest of the Vanaras, fell by his hand."

Ravana's eyes burned with pride and disdain. "I fear no man, no god. Let them come. I shall meet them with fire and steel."

But within the chambers of Ravana's mind, a storm began to brew. For though he spoke bravely, the omen of Rama's approach stirred something ancient in his soul—the whisper of fate.

Metaphysical Retelling: The Descent of Pride and the Approach of Integration

The Ruler of the Lower Self (**Ravana**) sat atop the throne of desire (**Lanka**), surrounded by advisors—fragments of the unintegrated mind. The psychic terrain trembled as the unified energies of devotion, discipline, and spiritual will—led by the incarnate Self (**Rama**), the king of higher nature—approached the gates of illusion.

The inner voices of arrogance, denial, and pride assembled in council.

The ruler of desire roared, "What force dares to challenge my sovereignty over the soul? Who disturbs the comfort of my dominion?"

A whisper from the subconscious spoke: "The Flame of the Self (**Rama**), joined by the disciplined will (**Lakshmana**), the awakened devotion (**Hanuman**), and the wild but loyal energies of mind (**Vanara host**), has crossed the ocean of separation. They approach on a bridge of intention, constructed by focused action."

One inner impulse scoffed: "What are these monkey-thoughts? Childish impulses! They cannot stand against the might of the ego."

But the cautious fragment—the deeper knowing—replied: "Do not mock what you fail to comprehend. These are not thoughts of the lower mind. These are qualities of transformation. Even pride has trembled before them."

The Desire-Mind (**Ravana**) bellowed in false confidence: "Let them come. I am lord of sensation, master of illusion. None shall dethrone me."

Yet within, a shiver stirred—a premonition. For the fortress of the lower self, long thought indestructible, had never faced a force so complete: a self-aware flame rising from the soul's own forgotten depth.

The approach of the Self was not an invasion. It was a reckoning.

Nala Constructs the Bridge to Lanka

(Source: Yuddha Kāṇḍa (Book of War), Chapter 30 – Nala Constructs the Bridge to Lanka)

Summary of Traditional Context:
After the ocean god refuses to yield, Rāma commands a solution. Nala, the son of the divine architect Vishvakarma, offers his inherited skill to build a bridge (Setu) to Lanka. The Vanaras, under his command, gather trees, rocks, and mountains to build the bridge. The sea calms in reverence, and the army of the Higher Self crosses the waters of illusion toward the battlefield of liberation.

The command of the exalted Self (Rāma) having been given, the divine host of awakened energies—the Vanaras (mental faculties), with joyful cries—gathered on the shore of the limitless ocean. Their task: to build a path of union between the fragmented self (Bharata's land) and the desire-bound soul (Lanka).

The flame of intellect known as Nala (a master of structure and divine architect) stepped forward and bowed to the incarnate Spirit. "O Light within," he said, "I carry within me the architectural seed of the Divine Builder, Vishvakarma. Permit me to construct the pathway across these waters."

With assent granted, Nala issued instructions. The mighty Vanaras, with hands skilled in gathering materials of the earth and sea, uprooted vast trees, carried mountain tops, and rolled great stones toward the roaring ocean. With strength and rhythm, the army of mind laid each piece like sacred syllables forming a mantra of return.

The ocean, once impassable, received their offering with calm. The waves grew still as if honoring the mission. Slowly, over days, a causeway appeared—stretching across the water like a divine breath uniting opposites.

Metaphysical Retelling: The Building of the Inner Bridge

When the Higher Self (Rāma) issues the inner command, the spiritual faculties (Vanaras)—which were once wild impulses—gather in harmony for a divine task. Their work is to build the inner pathway between the incarnate self and the soul imprisoned within the realm of desire (Lanka).

The Divine Architect within (Nala), a latent power of order and sacred design, steps forward. He represents the hidden structural memory within consciousness—the echo of the Cosmic Builder (Vishvakarma) encoded in the soul. He says to the Flame of Truth (Rāma):

"O Flame, I am fashioned after the Divine Pattern. The memory of sacred formation flows in me. Let me construct the bridge across the sea of separation."

Upon receiving approval, he calls forth the aligned faculties of thought and devotion. These faculties—once undisciplined—now work in sacred rhythm. They uproot the mental trees of belief, roll boulders of old tendencies, and repurpose them into tools of return.

Each step in building is a mantra. Each stone a spiritual principle placed with reverence.

The sea (symbol of the subconscious mind) accepts this act of will. The waves of emotion quiet. The bridge emerges—not merely as stone, but as a vibrational path across illusion.

The soul is no longer stranded. The return is underway.

Ravana's Panic and Preparations

(Source Reference: Yuddha Kāṇḍa, Chapter 31 of the Ramayana)

The Lower Nature Confronts the Force of Ascension

When Ravana (Desire-Mind) heard of the approaching army of Rama (Higher Self), his inner fortress trembled. Sitting in his jeweled hall within the golden city of Lanka (the astral-mental plane), his mind, full of pride and illusion, grew anxious.

Summoning his ministers, Ravana addressed them with frustration masked in royal calm:

"You have all witnessed my power. I have conquered gods and subdued elements. And yet, this human prince, Rama, marches with the Vanaras (mental forces), crossing oceans and bringing destruction. Tell me—what must we do now?"

At once, the ministers—servants of the lower nature—voiced praise and pride, reminding Ravana of his past victories. They spoke of how the divine armies had once fallen to his might and how his austerities had earned him boons even from Brahma.

But among them sat a voice of clarity—Vibhishana (Scientific Mind), his brother, who had not yet defected. He warned:

"Great king, do not underestimate this threat. Rama is no ordinary prince. He is dharma itself—righteousness incarnate. Return Sita (Buddhic Emotion-Nature). Make peace while it is still possible."

Ravana, caught between fear and arrogance, scorned the advice. His pride, like a ten-headed cloud, obscured reason. He ended the meeting in anger, his will now bent not on peace, but on defense and destruction.

Metaphysical Retelling: Ravana's Panic and Preparations

As the tidal wave of spiritual force approached, the ruler of the lower astral kingdom—the Desire-Mind (Ravana)—sat within the palace of illusion (Lanka), his many-headed intellect clouded with fear masked as fury. The Self (Rama) was advancing, not with physical soldiers, but with the awakened faculties of the mind, the refined thoughts, and the energies once trapped in ignorance, now marching toward truth.

Ravana (Desire-Mind) gathered the ministers of his psychic domain—the flatterers, rationalizers, and shadow-intellects that had once upheld his reign over the soul.

"You speak of the old victories," he said, "of how I (Desire-Mind) overcame even celestial forces (higher ideals). But this is no ordinary war. The Flame of the Self (Rama) comes now not as an abstraction, but embodied."

The ministers—extensions of ego, delusion, and pride—spoke in turn: "O king of form and sensation! You have mastered ascetic force. Your will conquered even heaven's decrees. None can match your might. This intruder is flesh—while you are fire."

Yet in that hall of shadows stood the Scientific Mind (Vibhishana), born of the same root as Desire but refined by reason and insight. And he spoke not with flattery, but truth:

"This Flame is not flesh. He is the Logos made manifest. He bears the arrow of intention, and every thought in his quiver is truth. Return the Soul (Sita) to its rightful center. Relinquish illusion. Redemption is still possible."

But the Desire-Mind, hardened through long sovereignty over the senses, rejected the counsel of reason. Pride, that ten-headed shadow, rose to drown the warning. The Scientific Mind was silenced—soon to depart for Light.

Thus did the lower nature choose conflict over surrender. Thus did it begin its descent toward dissolution.

THE BATTLE BETWEEN RAMA AND RAVANA

(Source Reference: Yuddha Kāṇḍa (Book of War), Chapter 59, of the Ramayana.)

The sun rose over the battlefield as Rama, the son of Dasharatha and avatar of Vishnu, stood facing Ravana, the ten-headed king of Lanka. The two great warriors were like cosmic opposites—Rama calm and radiant, Ravana furious and burning with desire.

Rama drew his bow, invoking the sacred mantras taught by the sages, while Ravana let out a terrifying roar that echoed across the skies. The armies of monkeys and rakshasas clashed below them as the two leaders prepared for their final duel.

Ravana hurled divine weapons, each filled with the power of destruction, but Rama—serene and unwavering—dispelled them with arrows of light and truth. The gods watched in awe as the battle of dharma and adharma unfolded in the skies and on the earth.

Lakshmana, Rama's loyal brother, had already struck down Indrajit, Ravana's son, with the help of Hanuman. Now, the fate of Lanka rested on this final confrontation.

With a voice like thunder, Ravana summoned his ultimate weapon—the Brahmastra. But Rama, holding the weapon of Vishnu, responded with divine precision. One by one, Ravana's heads were severed, only to grow back. But Rama understood the truth: each head represented a force within the desire-mind.

Finally, invoking the highest power of the Self, Rama fired the arrow gifted by Brahma. It pierced Ravana's heart. The ten-headed demon fell, not just slain—but liberated.

METAPHYSICAL RETELLING: THE FINAL CONFRONTATION OF SELF AND SHADOW

As the final stage of inner conflict approached, the Divine Self (Rama) stood before the fully matured distortion of the lower desire-mind (Ravana), the king of the inner Lanka—domain of passions and attachments.

The Self had descended far into matter, but now it faced the critical moment when the lower principle—disguised as grandeur, multiplicity, and power—would be challenged not by force, but by truth.

From the battlefield of the inner world, the mental faculties (Vanaras) and the unregenerate desires (Rakshasas) clashed wildly, yet the true battle was above—in the soul's firmament.

The lower mind (Ravana), with ten heads representing the fragmented sense-forces, unleashed a storm of illusion, but the Divine Self (Rama) remained poised. Each arrow fired was a focused intention, a vibration of spiritual discernment dissolving illusion.

The disciplined will (Lakshmana) had already neutralized the cunning distortions of self-deceit (Indrajit), and now stood as the guardian flame behind the Self.

The intellect awakened by the higher mind (Hanuman) bore the memory of the soul's purity and stood ready as a bridge between resolve and remembrance.

As the Self (Rama) observed the regenerating heads of the desire-mind (Ravana), it realized: this was not merely a demon to destroy—but a force to transmute. Only when the center of desire itself—the heart—was pierced by the flame of higher purpose, would transformation be complete.

So the Self called upon its divine source—its origin in the Logos (Brahma)—and summoned the arrow of final discernment. With one focused act of luminous will, it penetrated the core of illusion.

The lower nature collapsed, not as a victim of hate, but as a conquered distortion now returning to unity.

The battle ended. The soul was cleared. The Self had reclaimed the throne.

Sītā's Trial by Fire

(Source: Yuddha Kāṇḍa, Valmiki Ramayana, Chapter 68)

After the fall of Ravana, peace returned to the battlefield. The war was over. Rama stood victorious, but there remained a deeper trial—not one of weapons, but of truth.

Rama turned to Sītā, his wife, who had been held captive by Ravana in Lanka. Though his heart yearned for her, he expressed a solemn concern: her time spent in the house of another man might bring question to her purity in the eyes of the world.

Sītā, wounded by this implication, cried out in agony—not of guilt, but of being doubted by the one she loved. With great resolve, she called upon Agni, the god of fire, to bear witness to her purity. She declared she would undergo a trial by fire to prove her integrity.

A sacred pyre was lit. Without hesitation, Sītā stepped into the flames. But Agni, the divine fire, received her as a daughter and brought her forth unharmed, radiant and untouched. The gods themselves praised her. Rama accepted her back—not as property reclaimed, but as truth vindicated.

Thus, Sītā was restored—not just to Rama, but to her rightful place as the soul's intuitive light—now fully tested, purified, and whole.

Metaphysical retelling: Sītā's Trial by Fire

After the annihilation of the ten-headed distortion (Rāvaṇa), the Higher Self (Rāma)—the sovereign flame of divine order—stands not in celebration, but in solemn testing. This is not the end of a battle; it is the threshold of alchemical reunification between the soul and its spiritual essence. The scene is not a trial of a woman, but a cosmic ritual where the Buddhic light (Sītā)—the soul's divine purity and intuitive wisdom—must pass through the crucible of sacred fire (Agni), not for punishment, but for transmutation.

Why would the Higher Self demand that which is already pure to be tested?

Because in the journey of incarnation, even divine light passes through veils. The soul descends into form and enters the domain of distortion. Though untouched at its core, it must prove—to the remaining fragments of the personality and the collective subconscious—that it has not been tainted by the grasp of illusion (Rāvaṇa).

This ritual, then, is a metaphysical necessity.

The fire (Agni) represents the buddhic plane itself—pure discernment beyond duality, a plane where illusion cannot abide. It is not the fire of punishment but of verification. Agni, as the outpouring of spiritual activity from the atma-buddhi center (as described in the Ahavanīya fire), is the only force capable of recognizing what belongs to the Real.

Sītā steps into the fire not as a woman entering flames, but as the purified intuition re-entering the sacred light of higher awareness. Her passing through the fire is the Buddhic function reuniting with its source, showing that it was never truly lost—only veiled.

The fire, in return, lifts her—not in glory as a spectacle—but in vibrational affirmation: this soul is whole. The fire does not burn—it remembers. And in that remembrance, the inner faculties aligned with Rāma recognize her once again. It is not Rāma who doubts—it is the last remnants of fragmented perception in the lower nature that must now be reconciled.

The witnessing armies—the vanaras (primal forces) and rākṣasas (former distortions)—observe not an event, but a transmutation. Their gaze signifies the reconstitution of the psychic field. The battle within the soul is not complete until the Feminine Principle of the inner light—Buddhi as Sītā—is publicly recognized by all aspects of the psyche as untarnished, intact, and united with its source.

And why does Agni himself emerge as the deliverer?

Because Agni is the sacrificial force that bridges the mortal and divine. Agni is the channel through which offerings ascend. In this moment, Agni becomes the testimony—the medium through which the soul declares its purity. Agni is the bridge between Rāma and Sītā, between the spiritual ego and its intuitive light.

This is not a myth about fire or fidelity. This is a rite of return.

Sītā's emergence from the fire is the triumph of the Buddhic light over all karmic impressions, distortions, and projections. The inner feminine has walked through every temptation and has returned not only unharmed—but unveiled.

She is not purified by the fire. She is revealed through it.

This is how the Higher Self knows her. And this is how the soul, through its journey in form, comes to know itself—by walking through the sacred fire and emerging whole.

Arrival in Ayodhya and Descent from the Vimana

(Source: Book of War (Yuddha Kāṇḍa), Chapter 125)

As the celestial chariot (Pushpaka Vimana), radiant as the midday sun, approached the city of Ayodhya, all eyes were drawn toward the shimmering sky-path. Within the glowing vessel sat Rāma (the incarnate Self), Sītā (the purified buddhic soul), and Lakṣmaṇa (the disciplined Will), their journey through illusion nearing completion. The Vimana glided like thought itself, unimpeded, glorious with golden panels, encrusted gems, and tiny celestial bells ringing in subtle harmonies.

Rāma's gaze softened at the sight of his homeland. The city of Ayodhya, once shrouded in longing, now burst into joy. Crowds surged forth to greet the returning exiled prince. Bharata (moral conscience), who had ruled in abstinence, carrying Rāma's sandals upon the throne, now bowed low in reverence.

As the chariot descended, flowers rained from the sky and conches sounded. Sītā, veiled and serene, held a presence that silenced all doubts. The city's gates opened not merely in metal, but in hearts.

Rāma stepped down, crowned not yet by hand but by virtue. The people wept. The years of absence had only magnified their love. Mothers, elders, and warriors knelt before him. Then began the sacred rites, the cleansing waters, the white robes, and the golden ornaments, not as vanity but as tokens of a soul restored to wholeness.

In time, Rāma would ascend the throne—but in that moment, his very return was the coronation of Spirit over form, of Light over illusion.

Metaphysical Retelling: The Throne of the Self and The Descent of the Causal Flame

The Vimana is not merely a flying machine. It is the vehicle of the Causal Self—the perfected body of Light through which the Spirit travels once it has transmuted all lower tendencies. Rāma's descent upon Ayodhya is not spatial—it is a descent from higher consciousness into the heart of the soul.

Ayodhya, the "city without conflict," represents the inner sanctum—the soul aligned and free from duality. When Rāma returns, it symbolizes the final reintegration of the Self with its inner kingdom. This is the final phase of spiritual victory: enthronement.

The **Pushpaka Vimana**—crafted by divine architecture and responsive to thought—is the symbol of the **Causal Body**, or what some call the Light Body. It is the vehicle of the purified Self, free from karma, responsive only to intention, and resplendent with cosmic design. The **cat's-eye floors**, **golden lotuses**, **flags**, and **tiny bells** are not ornament—they are symbols: awakened perception, purity, spiritual sovereignty, and inner resonance.

When Rāma (the incarnate Atma-Buddhi) descends with Lakṣmaṇa (Individuality) and Sītā (the transfigured Soul), they descend not into geography, but into **conscious realization**. The descent from the Vimana is the final act of embodiment—when the perfected aspects of the self take residence in their rightful thrones within consciousness.

Bharata, who ruled by placing the shoes of Rāma upon the throne, represents the moral will preserving the space for divine rulership. The shoes are the advancing steps of Spirit—the power of return. Bharata symbolizes how **Duty bows before Love**, how the ego yields in reverence to the Self.

The coronation that follows is not merely ceremonial—it is alchemical. Rāma is now the sovereign of the inner kingdom. The **crown chakra opens**. The **soul (Sītā)** sits beside him. The **Will (Lakṣmaṇa)** guards the gates. And the **Intellect (Hanuman)**, having remembered its true power, stands in eternal bhakti.

This is the final transmutation—not of escape, but of divine dominion. Not of otherworldly disappearance, but of the **descent of Spirit into the vessel now made pure**.

THE RETURN OF THE SELF THROUGH THE CELESTIAL BODY (PUSHPAKA VIMANA)

(Source: Chapter 98–99 of the Yuddha Kāṇḍa)

Context: Rama prepares to return to Ayodhya after the defeat of Ravana, and Vibhishana presents him with the Pushpaka Vimana, a divine aerial chariot previously stolen from Kubera by Ravana.

After the victory was won and Lanka subdued, **Vibhishana**, the new lord of the Rakshasas, approached **Rama** with reverence. He spoke of the sacred chariot—the **Pushpaka Vimana**—a wondrous aerial vehicle that once belonged to **Kubera**, god of wealth, but had been seized by **Ravana** and was now in Vibhishana's possession.

"Let this celestial chariot bear you home," said Vibhishana. "It moves by thought, needs no reins, and shines like the golden sun."

Rama, however, hesitated. "My heart yearns for my brother **Bharata**, who renounced all comfort to rule in my name. Until I am reunited with him and my family—**Kausalya**, **Sumitra**, and even **Kaikeyi**—adornment and celebration do not please me."

Still, Vibhishana implored: "Let us honor you before your departure. Let the vanaras and warriors rest in joy after their trials. This moment is sacred."

Moved by the sincerity of his host, Rama consented. He, **Lakshmana**, **Sita**, and their companions ascended the radiant Pushpaka Vimana. The chariot sparkled with gold and crystal, chiming with celestial bells. As it rose, it hovered effortlessly in the sky, carrying the victors homeward.

Metaphysical Retelling: The Soul's Flight in the Causal Chariot

After the soul (Rama) had conquered its adversarial forces—desire (Ravana) and illusion (Lanka)—the faculty of refined intelligence, previously allied with lower thought but now turned to wisdom (Vibhishana), approached in reverence.

"O Radiance of the Inner Self (Rama)," said the purified mind (Vibhishana), "the celestial vehicle of divine memory and abundance (Pushpaka Vimana), once taken by the distorted desire-nature (Ravana), has been reclaimed. It is no ordinary vessel—it is the **Causal Body**, the subtle architecture of the soul built by divine Mind (Vishvakarma). It responds not to hands, but to Will."

The Higher Self replied: "My return to the moral center (Bharata)—the conscience who governed in my absence—is of utmost importance. The spiritual heart longs for its reunion. I must behold the moral essence that surrendered his comfort in faith, and my maternal archetypes—Compassion (Kausalya), Wisdom (Sumitra), and Karmic Law (Kaikeyi). Until this reunion, celebration holds no meaning."

But the awakened intellect pleaded: "Allow the faculties of the soul—the energies that toiled in the inner war—to rest in sacred stillness. Let the temple of the soul be adorned. Let devotion be shown not for ceremony's sake, but for love's acknowledgment."

Then the Flame of the Self (Rama) accepted. He, along with the Individuality (Lakshmana), the purified buddhic emotion-nature (Sita), and the hosts of integrated soul-forces (vanaras), boarded the Chariot of Light (Pushpaka Vimana).

And what was this Vimana?

It was not a machine—it was the causal body itself, formed by divine geometry and held together by purpose. Its golden pillars were the lotus-symbols of awakened potential. Its crystal floors were the pathways of insight. Its attics and mansions were the chambers of higher consciousness, ringing softly with the bells of awakened memory.

It was the Chariot of the Gods, reborn in the soul.

It did not fly across the sky as birds do—but across layers of mind, space, and time, rising beyond the lower planes toward the divine origin.

And in this moment, the Self (Rama) began his ascent—not merely to Ayodhya the city, but to **Ayodhya the state**—the realm of no conflict, where the crown of the Spirit (Sahasrara Chakra) awaits enthronement.

This is the Vimana within every seeker.

This is the body of light you are building with every act of purity, truth, and spiritual will.

It is not built of metal—but of memory.

Not powered by fire—but by intention.

You, too, shall board it when the inner war is won.

And when you do, may you rise—not outward, but inward—toward the throne of your true Self, where peace is not a promise, but a presence.

Rama Returns to Ayodhya and is Crowned King

Source: Ramayana – Book of War, Chapter 100 (Yuddha Kanda)

The Enthronement of the Self and the Opening of the Crown Chakra

After completing his long exile and the great war, the radiant Flame of the Self (Rama), along with the disciplined Will (Lakshmana), the intuitive Soul-light (Sita), and the army of purified energies, ascended the celestial chariot (Pushpaka Vimana) that soared through the skies like thought itself. The chariot moved at the speed of divine intention, shining like a sun in motion, directed not by reins but by will.

As they approached the gates of the inner kingdom (Ayodhya), great anticipation stirred in the hearts of the people. The citizens, sages, ministers, and the moral essence of the Self (Bharata), who had governed in the Self's absence, gathered in joy and reverence.

The Flame (Rama) descended with glory, greeted by the aspects of Divine Motherhood—Love (Kausalya), Wisdom (Sumitra), and Karma (Kaikeyi)—who embraced the returning soul in full forgiveness and integration.

The disciplined Will (Lakshmana) stood beside him. The Soul-light (Sita), now refined through the fire of trials, walked with grace. The Breath of Devotion (Hanuman) bowed low, unwilling to accept any throne or gift, asking only to serve eternally at the feet of the Self.

The soul's throne awaited.

Then the great anointing took place.

Waters from sacred rivers—symbols of awakened consciousness—were poured upon the crown of the Self (Rama), while hymns of eternal praise echoed in the inner world. Saffron robes, ornaments of divine qualities, and garlands of spiritual truth adorned the Self.

The Flame (Rama) was enthroned.

The kingdom of the soul was once again aligned.

Metaphysical Retelling: The Enthronement of the Higher Self in the Inner Kingdom

After the descent into matter, the battle with distortion, and the retrieval of the lost Light (Sita), the Higher Self (Rama) prepares to reclaim dominion over the inner world. Riding the Causal Body (Pushpaka Vimana)—a perfected mental-spiritual vehicle that responds to intention alone—the Self begins the ascent back to the divine center of consciousness (Ayodhya).

Each element of the inner psyche rejoices: the intellect, the emotions, the instincts, the elders (ancient patterns), and the pure moral essence (Bharata) who has safeguarded the throne in the soul's absence. Bharata represents the soul's original alignment to truth—still seated in dharma, waiting not to rule but to restore the true ruler.

As the Self returns, it is embraced by the Trinity of Divine Forces that govern incarnation: the Mother of Compassion (Kausalya), the Mother of Wisdom (Sumitra), and the Mother of Consequence (Kaikeyi). These archetypal mothers are not figures of drama—but spiritual forces that bring karma, guidance, and love into incarnation.

The Will (Lakshmana) stands guard—the unwavering companion of the Self throughout trials.

The purified Soul-Light (Sita), who has endured the fire of testing and emerged whole, walks by the Self's side. She is no longer merely receptive—but radiant, sovereign, and whole.

The Breath of the Soul (Hanuman), embodiment of unshakable devotion, kneels—not for reward, but for continued service. He refuses gifts, wealth, or status—only asking to live in remembrance of the Self. This is the perfected prāṇic force, dedicated to carrying out divine will across all realms.

Then comes the coronation—not a political event, but the activation of the Crown Chakra.

Waters from all sacred rivers—the streams of awakened spiritual consciousness—are poured on the crown of the Self. These waters descend through lifetimes, gathering power from rivers of memory, karma, and divine purpose. As they fall, the inner temple is cleansed.

Adorned in saffron—the flame of renunciation—and in gold—the light of divine purity—the Self sits upon the throne of inner equilibrium.

This is the moment of **realization**.

The Self is re-enthroned not only in the psyche, but in the cosmic order. Harmony is restored. The Flame of the Self now governs, not by force—but by the resonance of divine being. His throne is not in a palace—but in the purified heart.

The return to Ayodhya is the return to the state of union, where the Soul, the Self, the Will, and the Breath are one.

This is not a story—it is a state.

And so ends the War—not with bloodshed, but with the crowning of clarity.

Indra and Vṛtra – The Battle of the Hidden Waters

There was once a time when the streams of divine truth—symbolized as celestial waters—were held back, locked away by the force of concealment, inertia, and ignorance. This force took the form of **Vṛtra**, whose name means "the Encloser." He was not merely a demon, but a symbol of the closed gates of perception, the constriction of soul currents, and the veil wrapped around higher truth. Vṛtra was the crystallized resistance in the astral and lower mental planes, hoarding the waters of illumination meant for the unfolding soul.

And who rose to confront him?

It was **Indra**, "the thousand-eyed," the Will of the Divine operating through awakened perception. But Indra is not a god in the common sense—he is the Divine Will, born of devotion and earnest spiritual effort. He is that resolute spiritual faculty in the evolving being that reaches upward, seeking to shatter illusion and liberate the latent light.

Indra does not move alone. He arises when the soul reaches the threshold of its next initiation—when the **Devayāna**, the Path of the Gods, begins to open. This is the phase where the Monad of Life begins to overshadow the monad of form, marking the entry into higher planes of evolution.

Before the battle, Indra must first receive the energy of **Soma**—the divine nectar of inspired consciousness. Soma is not a physical drink, but the spiritual ambrosia drawn down through meditation, devotion, and moral clarity. It is this inner anointing that activates the Will into a force of liberation.

Armed with **the thunderbolt** (vajra), which is not a weapon of destruction but of discriminative illumination, Indra ascends. The thunderbolt is the lightning strike of truth that disintegrates veils and cleaves apart falsehood. It is pure will powered by inner vision.

The battle unfolds not in the outer world, but in the subtle realms of the soul. **Vṛtra** represents every block in the nadis (energy channels), every hardened fear in the emotional body, every false belief guarding the gates of inner waters. **Indra**, as the will devoted to the higher, strikes—not with anger, but with unwavering clarity.

And when the blow lands, **the waters burst forth**.

These waters are not H2O—they are **the two streams of heavenly truth and purity**. The metaphysical twin currents that flow from Atma-Buddhi, symbolized in the ancient scriptures as the streams falling on the head of the newborn Buddha. They are the illumination of the higher mind and the cleansing of the desire nature. They wash the soul clean, lifting the veils that once made heaven appear distant.

In the aftermath, the soul does not merely drink of the waters—it becomes the channel. It becomes a singer of light—one of the **pious Singers**, the Maruts, who rejoice in harmony and descend into incarnation by free will. These Singers, divine sparks, now echo the wisdom from the cornerstone of Being, singing alongside the **morning stars**, the harmonized mental faculties.

In this moment, the **personality** begins to realize it is not the master but the vessel. The causal-self—that high seat of memory, will, and divine imagination—begins to emanate through. It is through this act that **Indra** becomes more than an energy—he becomes a gateway.

As the **Gārhapatya Fire** (symbol of spiritual activity in the causal-body) is rekindled, the soul begins to build its resurrection body, life after life, ascending through the **Devayāna** toward ultimate union with the Brahmanic flame.

Thus, this story is not about gods clashing in heaven—it is a map of liberation, a tale of the Will of God within the soulbreaking open the dam of illusion so that truth may once again circulate freely through the body, mind, and spirit.

This is the first test of the initiate: to unleash the Divine Will through devotion and clarity, and to face and overcome the soul's internal Vṛtra.

Indra's Fall from Heaven – The Descent of the Divine Will into Self-Reflection

Mythic Context:
In Vedic mythology, **Indra**, the sovereign of the heavens, once committed a transgression—typically an act of arrogance or desire—and was cast down from his celestial throne. In various tales, his fall is brought about by pride, forgetfulness of dharma, or indulgence in sensual pleasure. Often humiliated, stripped of his powers, or pursued by curses, he is forced into retreat, purification, and redemption. The loss of Indra's heavenly seat symbolizes a disruption in the cosmic order—one where the representative of Divine Will has violated its own law.

Let us now reframe this through metaphysical vision, using the definitions you provided:

Metaphysical Retelling

When the Divine Will (**Indra**) forgets its source in the Absolute, it begins to turn inward, not in contemplation—but in self-glorification.

Once born of earnest striving and devotion to the Highest, the Will now assumes authority for its own sake. It claims heaven not as a reflection of divine law, but as a personal possession. This shift, though subtle, fractures the balance.

For **Indra** is not merely strength—he is the Devoted Will to Divine Order. His thousand eyes do not belong to him; they are borrowed lenses through which the cosmos observes itself in all directions. But when those eyes close to the inner sun, the radiance dims.

Thus begins **the fall**.

The Will that once soared across **Devayāna**, the Path of the Gods—ascending through the realms of **Agni** (spiritual fire), **Vayu** (thought), **Varuṇa** (truth), **Prajāpati** (direct vision), and **Brahman** (pure spirit)—now collapses downward through its own self-interference.

Stripped of its elevation, Indra plunges from his throne in **Svarga** (heaven), and the soul experiences a **loss of authority over its inner planes**.

It is at this moment that the personality (**King Nada**) begins to rise. When the Will is dethroned, the egoic self, no longer restrained, takes the scepter. And so begins the drama of karmic rebalance.

But even in this fall, **Indra does not perish**—for he is still **Ahavanīya**, the sacrificial fire that never fully extinguishes. He retreats into the **Gārhapatya fire**—the causal-body's innermost sanctuary—and begins the long journey of re-sanctification.

The Fall of Indra is not punishment—it is the **soul's confrontation with self-will**.

In the descent, the Will witnesses the distortion it created. The **People**—symbols of the lower mind and untrained emotions—mock the fallen king. **The banners of the city** flutter in triumph, representing the rise of public opinion and external authority over inner spiritual direction.

It is in this pit of reversal that Indra is forced to **reconsecrate himself**. He must bathe again in the **Water from Heaven**—the twin streams of **Truth and Purity** flowing from **Atma-Buddhi**—to regain clarity. Until then, the **Doorkeepers of Brahman**—his own aspects of Will and Vision (Indra and Prajāpati)—stand silent at the gates.

The once outward Will must become inwardly devoted again. The ego must surrender to the deeper Self.

And thus, Indra must earn his heaven once more—not through might, but through **Devotion**, **Penance**, and **Illumined Humility**.

He must become the **servant of Dharma**, not its enforcer.

He must bow before the Flame he once wielded.

Then, and only then, will he rise again—not to rule, but to reflect the **true sovereignty of the Causal Self**, which is neither above nor below, but within.

The Thunderbolt of Awakening – Indra's Lightning and the Birth of the Mind

In Vedic lore, **Indra**, lord of the Devas, wields a mighty weapon known as **Vajra**, the thunderbolt. With it, he slays **Vṛtra**, the serpent of obstruction who hoards the celestial waters. When Vṛtra is vanquished, the waters flow freely again, and light returns to the world.

But this is not merely the story of a god smiting a dragon—it is the sacred allegory of how the spiritual mind is born.

Metaphysical Retelling:

There once was a time when the soul—descended into matter—lost access to its higher faculties. The waters of divine intuition and inner clarity were dammed, locked away by **Vṛtra**, the coiled force of resistance. This serpent was not evil—it was **obstruction** itself: the inertia of the subconscious, the layers of accumulated ignorance that bury the Self.

In this dim twilight, the soul wandered through shadows, blind to its origin, thirsty for truth.

Then came **Indra**, not as an outer savior, but as the **inner Will-to-Know**, the uprising of divine remembrance within. He is the awakened current in the soul that declares: "I was not born to crawl."

In his right hand, he carries **Vajra**—not a weapon of destruction, but a **flash of knowing**—a ray of divine mind. The Vajra is the sharpened clarity of higher consciousness, forged from the friction of aspiration and discipline. It is the **diamond-point of mental illumination**, cutting through the veils of delusion.

When Indra strikes Vṛtra with the Vajra, the serpent is split—not slain in vengeance, but **opened**. The coils of resistance unwind, and the **celestial waters**—symbolizing the **flow of spiritual knowledge, intuition, and divine nourishment**—pour forth.

This moment is the **birth of the illumined mind**.

It is not that Indra kills the serpent—it is that the Will, aligned with the Spirit, **penetrates the barrier** of darkness and releases the soul's inner light.

The Symbolism of Vajra:

- **Vajra** means both thunderbolt and diamond. It is the paradox of force and clarity, power and permanence.

- It represents the **invincible mind**—not intellect in the worldly sense, but the Buddhic-intellect illuminated by the fire of the Atman.

- When wielded by the true Indra within (the divine Will), Vajra becomes the **power to pierce**

falsehood, to awaken the higher faculties, to reestablish the soul's sovereignty over itself.

Inner Alchemy:

The story of Indra and Vajra is **the story of every initiate**.

- Vṛtra is the **lower mind**, the accumulation of karmic impressions, fear, confusion.

- Indra is the **causal Will** purified by devotion and truth-seeking.

- Vajra is the **point of awakening**—the moment the soul remembers who it is.

- The released waters are the **unlocked faculties** of inspiration, inner vision, creativity, and divine communion.

When the strike happens, it is not violent. It is inevitable.

For when the Will aligns with the Truth, the barriers must fall. The serpent does not die—it **transforms**. That which once hoarded the waters becomes the channel through which they flow.

Application for the Initiate:

This myth reminds the aspirant:

- You do not slay your darkness—you illumine it.

- Your greatest weapon is not force—but **focused clarity**.

- The thunderbolt is not out there—it is the **light of inner realization**.

- The waters you seek—love, peace, wisdom—are **already within you**, awaiting release.

You are Indra when you will to rise.
You are Vajra when you pierce illusion.
You are the soul when you remember the **light you forgot you were**.

The Palace of the Ego and the Arrival of the Architect – Indra and Viśvakarma

Mythic Context:
Having conquered the worlds and established his throne as King of the Gods, **Indra** (Divine Will) desired a palace so magnificent it would reflect his cosmic supremacy. He commissioned the great divine architect **Viśvakarma**, who built a palace of dazzling proportions. But Indra's desire grew insatiable—he kept asking for more rooms, more grandeur, more halls. Eventually, the architect prayed for deliverance from this endless task. Then arrived **a child-sage**—a mysterious Brahmin—who gently revealed to Indra the futility of his quest by telling him that countless Indras have come and gone before, each thinking themselves supreme.

Now we unveil the sacred metaphysics hidden within this legend.

Metaphysical Retelling: The House that Ego Built

The Divine Will (**Indra**) emerged from victory—not over others, but over its own ignorance. Yet what follows spiritual conquest is the most subtle danger: **the inflation of self-righteousness**.

Having ascended through devotion and fire, the Will turned to create a **structure to house its glory**. Not satisfied with stillness, the Will sought reflection in form. Thus it called upon **Viśvakarma**, the Divine Architect—**the blueprinting faculty of Divine Mind**.

Viśvakarma began to build—not of stone or silver, but of archetypal structure: walls of intention, floors of consecrated will, corridors of harmonized thought.

At first, the Will was pleased.

But soon, it wanted more.

Not content with the spiritual skeleton, **Indra desired immortality in structure**, permanence in matter. The palace grew. The Self became more invested in what it was building than in what it was becoming. The Will hardened into pride.

And so, **Viśvakarma**, the inner architect, wearied.

He who reflects **divine proportion**, who aligns **inner space with cosmic law**, could no longer build without violating the truth. He prayed for a higher correction. He knew: this was no longer creation—it was aggrandizement.

Then came **the Cosmic Child**—a sage of immeasurable age, clothed in youth.

The child entered Indra's palace and gently smiled. He admired the splendor, but spoke of previous palaces—infinitely more glorious—that had been built by Indras now forgotten. He said: "This palace will fall like theirs, for every flame must return to its wick, and every form to its formless source."

He gestured to **an ant** crawling across the floor, and said: "This one was once an Indra too."

With those words, **the veil shattered**.

The Will awoke to its own illusion. It saw that even in spiritual attainment, ego can disguise itself as divinity. And that permanence lies not in structure, but in the unstructured.

Thus the palace was abandoned—not in shame, but in liberation.

Indra laid down his crown, not to reject rulership, but to embrace humility.

He did not cease to be the Divine Will—he became its servant.

And **Viśvakarma**, the Architect, smiled again—for now he could build not for pride, but for **purpose**.

From this point onward, the soul would never again seek heaven in buildings of thought—but in **the unbuilded Temple of the Heart**, whose blueprints are drawn by Silence, and whose cornerstone is **remembrance of the Eternal**.

The Path of Return – Indra and the Devayāna

Mythic Context (Upanishadic Reference):
In the sacred scriptures, particularly the Kaushitaki Upanishad (I.2), it is said that the soul who has reached the **Devayāna**, the path of the gods, begins a journey through realms of increasing brilliance. This path includes stages: **the world of Agni (fire)**, **Vāyu (air)**, **Varuṇa (truth)**, **Indra (devotion and will)**, **Prajāpati (creative wisdom)**, and finally **Brahman (the Absolute Spirit)**. Indra, in this sacred sequence, is not a destination, but **a gatekeeper**—a phase of realization that the seeker must pass through to reach the formless Divine.

Metaphysical Retelling: The Divine Will as a Gatekeeper of Light

When the soul awakens from the long slumber of desire and descent, it does not immediately arrive at God—it ascends through **rays of its own forgotten greatness**, stages of remembering what it once was.

This ascent is known to the ancients as **Devayāna**—the shining pathway walked not by the flesh, but by the eternal essence clothed in light.

Here, **Indra**, no longer the egoic king, becomes the **flaming Will of Ascent**, a divine quality that both tests and empowers the soul. He is the fire of devotion, the sharp edge of direction, and the internal voice that whispers, "Rise."

As the soul enters the **world of Agni**, it becomes aware of its own inner combustion. The lower is sacrificed—burned—so that the Higher may emerge. This is the baptism by fire, where desire is transmuted into aspiration.

Then comes the **world of Vāyu**, the breath of God—the motion of thought purified by the wind of detachment. The soul learns to move without grasping, to flow without fixing.

It rises to the **world of Varuṇa**, the keeper of Truth. Here, every falsehood—every mask—is stripped away. The soul must gaze into the waters of its own subconscious and face the mirror of divine law.

Only then does it approach **Indra**, not as the king of heaven, but as **the flame of purified Will**. He stands now as the **Doorkeeper of Dharma**, the initiator into the Hall of the Eternal.

Indra tests the soul not with battle, but with stillness. He asks: "Do you seek power, or union? Dominion, or surrender?"

Those who answer with silence pass through.

For Indra is not the final station, but a **threshold**—the balancing point between mastery and humility. His presence dissolves ambition into **directionless devotion**.

And then the soul approaches **Prajāpati**, the Divine Architect—wisdom personified, who speaks not in words, but in form. Here the soul sees the cosmic pattern, the symmetry of Self within Self, the harmony of all lives woven into one.

At last, the soul rises to **Brahman**—the Unnamed, the Unspeakable.

The Path of the Gods ends in **no-form**, and yet in **All-Being**.

But remember: this entire journey is internal.

The world of fire is your suffering.
The wind is your shifting thoughts.
The waters are your heart.
The Will is your Indra.
The Wisdom is your higher Mind.
And Brahman is your **own sacred stillness**, from which you fell—and to which you now return.

Indra, then, is no longer the destination, nor the ego. He is the **inner flame of upward movement**, the electric current of soul that demands evolution.

This is the **real coronation** of Indra: not as king of heavens, but as **Servant of the Way**—the guardian of souls climbing toward the Absolute.

Indra's Journey Along the Devayāna

The Ascent of the Will through the Inner Planes

"Having reached the Path of the Gods, the man comes to the world of Agni, to the world of Vāyu, to the world of Varuṇa, to the world of Indra, to the world of Prajāpati, and to the world of Brahman."
— Kaushitaki Upanishad I.2

Mystical Narrative: The Will's Journey into the Infinite

There is a path—ancient, golden, and invisible to mortal senses—called **Devayāna**, the Way of the Gods. It is not traversed by feet, nor measured in miles. It begins when the seeker no longer clings to the shadows of the world, but turns inward, into the temple of light.

And at the root of that ascent stands **Indra**, the Will—not willfulness, not ambition, but that inner divine force which says: **"I must return."**

This chapter unveils Indra not as king of lightning alone, but as **the ascending current of spiritual fire** that carries the soul through the inner heavens. His journey is the soul's journey—the **Will of the Self** threading upward through its own forgotten hierarchy.

Stage One: The World of Agni – The Sacrifice of Desire

Indra's journey begins in the blazing chamber of **Agni**, where the inner fire tests all that is false. This fire is not destruction—it is transformation. It consumes the ego's demands and forges the purity required for higher light. Here the Will learns surrender—not to weakness, but to truth.

This is the birth of Indra within: when the soul chooses to burn for the sake of its own purification.

Stage Two: The World of Vāyu – The Breath of Detachment

The next stage is the airy realm of **Vāyu**, where thought no longer clings. Here, Indra becomes the breath of awareness moving freely across the mind. In this world, the soul releases its fixation on form, and learns to drift in the **space between certainty**.

Vāyu teaches Indra how to flow without losing direction— how to balance freedom with focused ascent.

Stage Three: The World of Varuṇa – The Mirror of Truth

Now the Will confronts the ocean of **Varuṇa**, the god of cosmic order and inner transparency. Every illusion must be seen, every hidden corner of the psyche revealed. The soul now gazes into the deep waters of the subconscious and is shown not only what it is—but what it is becoming.

Here, Indra is tested not by outer enemies, but by the fear of inner truth.

Stage Four: The World of Indra – The Flame of Steadfast Devotion

Having passed through the fires of will, the winds of thought, and the waters of truth, the Will meets itself—**Indra meets Indra**. At this gate, the Will becomes devotion. No longer a force for personal achievement, it is now a **servant of the Highest**.

Indra becomes the flame that bows to the Absolute. It is the **Will spiritualized**, no longer asserting, but aligning.

Here the Self is no longer climbing—it is being drawn upward.

Stage Five: The World of Prajāpati – The Pattern of the Logos

Then comes **Prajāpati**, the Lord of Creation, who holds the blueprints of form. In this world, the Will is shown the symmetry of all life, the unity of archetypes, the divine mathematics that bind stars and souls.

Indra here receives **vision**—not of what he wants, but of how he fits.

The Will sees its own limitation dissolve into **cosmic participation**. It becomes a ray of the universal mind.

Stage Six: The World of Brahman – The Formless Flame

Finally, the Will dissolves into the **Pure Spirit**—Brahman, the Unspoken Source. Here, all identity ceases. Even the divine Will no longer strives, no longer affirms, but becomes a silent pulse of radiance in the Infinite.

Indra vanishes into stillness.

The ascension completes in **disappearance**—not of existence, but of separation. The Will is no longer "a god." It is now **God-being**.

Metaphysical Insight: What This Journey Means for Us

The journey of Indra along the Devayāna is not a myth—it is **your map**.

It teaches us that:

- **Desire must be burned** (Agni)
- **Thought must be freed** (Vāyu)
- **Truth must be faced** (Varuṇa)
- **Devotion must guide Will** (Indra)
- **Vision must transcend ego** (Prajāpati)
- **Union must replace identity** (Brahman)

To walk this path is to become the inner Indra—**not a warrior**, but a flame.
Not a ruler, but a servant of truth.
Not a seeker of light, but light itself returning home.

This is the true coronation of Indra within the soul.

The Twin Guardians of the Inner Palace – Indra, Yama, and the Seat of the Causal Self

Mythic Prelude:

In the Kaushītaki Upanishad, the soul, upon departing from the mortal coil and ascending through the higher planes, arrives at a luminous threshold—the **Hall of Brahman**, the dwelling of the Supreme.

At its entrance stand **two divine guardians**: **Indra**, the god of thunder and vision, and **Prajāpati**, the Lord of Creation (in some versions, **Yama**, the god of Death and Judgment). The soul must approach them before entering the "palace of perfection."

But in a higher reading, this is not a tale of death. This is the secret of **self-transcendence**—of passing from the mortal personality into the eternal Causal Self, the immortal inner body of divine memory and realization.

Metaphysical Retelling

The aspirant—after lifetimes of purification, insight, and sacrifice—draws near to the gateway of the true Self, the eternal Temple of Light. This temple is not above the heavens, but **within**. It is the sanctuary of Tajjalān, the One from whom all things come, dwell, and return.

At the gateway stand **Indra** and **Yama**—not as external deities, but as **inner sentinels** guarding the **Causal**

Body(kāraṇa-śarīra), the resurrection body of the soul formed by accumulated truth, wisdom, and divine striving.

- **Indra** here is not simply willpower—but **Divine Will illuminated by vision**, the Self's luminous urge toward the eternal.

- **Yama** is not the fearsome judge—but the **perfected Personality**, now transfigured into a vessel of eternal memory. He is death conquered, the lower self made sacred and returned to the Light.

These two are the **Doorkeepers of Truth**.

But in this sacred narrative, something extraordinary occurs:

"He approaches the doorkeepers Indra and Prajāpati… and they run away from him."
— Kaushītaki Upanishad, I.2

Why do they flee?

Because the soul has **outgrown them**.

When the aspirant becomes **one with Divine Will** (Indra) and has **perfected the lower personality** (Yama), the dual guardians are no longer gatekeepers—they are qualities already embodied. They no longer test—they **bow**. The soul no longer seeks entry—it **is the temple**.

This is the inner alchemy of deification.

The Causal Self Revealed:

Upon entering the **Hall of Brahman**, the soul no longer identifies with body or emotion, desire or fear. It awakens as the **Causal Self**—a body of pure knowing, memory, and light. The Causal Body is:

- The **inner vesture** of the Divine Ego (ātma-buddhi-manas).

- The **vessel of continuity** through countless incarnations.

- The **ark of sacred memory**, where all spiritual victories are preserved and woven into form.

- The **Vimāna**—the chariot of light which carries the Self across lives, not by movement through space, but through states of consciousness.

Indra and Yama Within:

- **Indra** (Ahavanīya Fire) is the radiant will that burns upward in sacrifice.

- **Yama** (Gārhapatya Fire) is the stable center of being, the soul's hearth, the perfected pattern of the lower self.

Together, they are the **two fires** that converge in the **Agnihotra**—the ritual of Self-offering.

In the mature soul, these fires no longer burn separately—
they **merge into the flame of liberation**.

Mystical Insight:

This story is not about death.
It is about **resurrection before death**.

You, the reader, are **already journeying** toward the hall. Each moment of courage, each act of love, each selfless thought is another step upward.

- When **your will** becomes indistinguishable from Divine Will, you have met Indra.

- When **your personality** becomes purified of ego and bears the stamp of eternal truth, you have met Yama.

- When **you are both**, the guardians part—and you awaken within the Palace.

This is not a metaphor. This is a blueprint.

You are the traveler, the temple, and the throne.

Indra's Benediction — The Completion of the Soul's Descent

After the great war had ended, and the embodiment of Divine Order (Rāma) had conquered the tenfold illusion of desire (Rāvaṇa), the gods themselves descended upon the purified field of action. Among them came the Lord of the Celestial Forces, the thousand-eyed seer of the heavens, Indra. Clad in luminous armor and crowned with wisdom gained through trials of spiritual will, Indra approached Rāma, his gaze steady and eternal.

"O Radiant Son of the Solar Flame," said Indra, "you have redeemed the world from the coils of distortion. Ask now any boon, and it shall be granted."

The Warrior of Truth, still radiant from battle, but never intoxicated by victory, bowed slightly and said, "Let those who have perished in devotion to the Higher Path—those divine beasts of strength and the loyal souls of Earth—be restored to life. Let no sacrifice go without the gift of remembrance."

Indra, moved by this request which bore no self-interest, raised his hand. "It is done," he declared. "All those whose breath ended in this holy war shall rise again. Not by desire, but by righteousness, are they restored."

A hush fell over the heavenly host as the field itself shimmered. The winds whispered of resurrection. The mountain base and forest crowns stirred gently, and the souls of the fallen rose—renewed, not as they were, but as they had become: clear, radiant, and free.

Part Two: The Metaphysical Retelling - The Reunion of Will and Solar Flame

After the spiritual Self (Rāma) had shattered the tenfold illusion of desire-bound intellect (Rāvaṇa), the forces of the higher mind—celestial archetypes who govern spiritual perception—descended into the field of inner silence. Among them stood Divine Will itself (Indra), the thousand-eyed faculty of higher vigilance, earned through unwavering devotion and disciplined ascension.

Indra, the Guardian of Heaven's Path, stepped forward and addressed the Soul-Flame incarnate:

"O embodiment of Divine Harmony, you have reconciled the fragmented self and pierced the veil of shadow. Ask what you will."

The Flame of the Self (Rāma), though complete in purpose, spoke not for himself but for the soul's companions—those animal aspects, primal energies, and loyal faculties that surrendered themselves in service to Light:

"Let them rise again. Let the instincts that bowed to Spirit, the urges that once roared in confusion but were redirected by will, be given resurrection—not as beasts, but as awakened aspects of Selfhood."

Then Divine Will (Indra) extended its authority: "So shall it be. Every part of the lower being that surrendered to the greater design shall return—not to repeat the old life, but to ascend with the new light."

And so, in the soul's inner landscape, a resonance emerged. The subtle bodies stirred. What had been sacrificed was not lost—it was refined, reclaimed, and reawakened as purified force. Thus, the boon of Indra is not reward, but recognition. Not a prize, but a return to cosmic alignment.

The Awakening of the Petrified Soul – The Liberation of Ahalyā

Part One: Sacred Narrative

Long ago, in the hermitage of Gautama the Sage, there lived Ahalyā—born of divine grace, radiant with inner light. Her beauty was said to rival the dawn. One day, while her consort was away deep in meditation, the Lord of Heaven, Indra—desiring her light—disguised himself in the form of her husband and approached her.

Though the nature of the encounter varies across traditions—some calling it seduction, others deception—it is said that Ahalyā, either deceived or compliant, was touched by the celestial king. When the sage returned, he saw through the illusion and pronounced a curse upon Ahalyā, turning her into stone—not out of anger, but to conceal her light until it could be awakened by divine fire.

Ages passed…

Then came Rāma, the flame of dharma, walking the path of exile. As his foot touched the hermitage, a wave of sacred resonance awakened the ground itself. The petrified Ahalyā was released from her slumber. Her form returned, her light restored—not merely as she was, but transfigured. The sage, too, returned and forgave her, knowing that her ordeal was part of a greater unfolding. Ahalyā bowed before Rāma, offering reverence—not to a man, but to the inner light that dispels illusion.

Part Two: Metaphysical Interpretation - The Descent of Will and the Reawakening of the Soul's Purity

Within the deeper chambers of the soul lives Ahalyā—the pristine aspect of the intuitive mind, untainted by desire yet exposed to its currents. She is the untouched Light, but not yet anchored in discernment. In this myth, Ahalyā represents the **buddhic purity** within the causal body— still latent, not fully awakened, but radiating an invisible perfection.

The Sage Gautama, her divine consort, represents **Spiritual Wisdom**—that which holds the Light in sacred alignment. But when Wisdom withdraws (meditates), even the purest aspects of the Self can fall prey to distortion.

Enter Indra—not as villain, but as the **Divine Will** misapplied. His thousand eyes symbolize expansive perception, but without centered harmony, Will can impersonate Wisdom. Indra's act is not carnal—it is symbolic of the soul's **first misuse of higher force** in the lower realms. The result is fragmentation: the Light (Ahalyā) is buried, concealed beneath the stone of karmic dormancy.

The "stone" is not punishment—it is preservation. It is the soul held in stasis until it can be awakened **not by doctrine, but by Presence**.

Then comes **Rāma**, the Flame of the Higher Self, walking the path of exile—that is, moving through the dense planes of human experience. His arrival is not physical—it is vibrational. When his foot touches the earth (symbol of embodiment), the buried Light stirs. Rāma does not "liberate" Ahalyā—**he recognizes her**.

Recognition is the key.

The moment the Higher Self beholds the buddhi—no longer as an ideal, but as a living fire—it is reanimated. The soul is no longer frozen in illusion. It returns not as victim, but as master of its own purity.

Ahalyā's bow before Rāma is not subservience—it is **surrender of the lower identity** to the Logos within. The Sage, representing Wisdom, returns to her not in wrath but in union. Will, Light, and Wisdom are reconciled in the eternal hermitage of the Self.

RAMA Chapter 7

BRAHMAN: The First Flame of All - Who is Brahman Metaphysically

Brahman is the eternal and unconditioned reality, the unmanifest Source from which all manifestation springs and into which all form dissolves. It is not a being, but Being itself—without boundary, without origin, without duality. Brahman is not to be grasped by the senses nor bound by name or form. It is pre-essence—the Infinite Flame that neither arises nor perishes, yet gives rise to all cycles, all forms, and all movements of the soul.

Brahman is the Self beyond self—the indivisible Unity that is both the Silence before all sound and the Voice that utters all creation. It is the Source of life, yet not life as we know it, but **Life as Divine Stillness**, the unmoved Mover, the Infinite Ether that both contains and transcends every cosmos. It is the heart of the Real, untouched by division, untouched by time, untouched by becoming.

All gods, all selves, all energies are emanations of this central Flame. Yet Brahman remains unborn, unthinkable, unspeakable. It is not fixed, and it cannot be grasped even by the highest intellect. It is **the beyond of all categories**, the unmoving essence from which all motion flows. To know Brahman is not to think it, but to become silence before its radiance.

And yet, this unknowable Supreme does not withhold itself—it breathes itself into form, becoming the soul in man, the light in the sun, the pulse of galaxies, and the still eye within the heart. He who sees all as Brahman sees no division, no other, no fear. For the self and the Supreme are one, and this One is Brahman—the groundless ground of all.

The Unnamed Flame before Flame

(LAYER 1: The ABSOLUTE)

To understand Brahman, one must behold the Absolute—not as an object of knowledge, but as the ineffable foundation from which knowledge, knower, and known emerge. The Absolute is not a being among beings; it is pre-being, the rootless root from which the tree of all manifestation grows.

It is pure potentiality—prior to thought, prior to light, prior to even the gods. It is not essence, but the principle from which essence is born. In this light, Brahman is seen as the **revelation of the Absolute**—its radiant face when it chooses to shine into time.

Just as the sun cannot be separated from its light, Brahman cannot be separated from the Absolute. But the Absolute remains unmanifest, unknowable, and veiled in what the sages called "thrice-unknown Darkness." It is the stillness from which Brahman moves—the pure silence from which the voice of the cosmos is spoken.

Thus, Brahman is the speakable edge of the Absolute—the first breath of the Eternal into form, the infinite Sea becoming wave, that It may know Itself in reflection.

The Womb of Sound, the Body of Brahman

(LAYER 2: AKĀŚA)

To approach Brahman more deeply, we must pass through the veil of **Akāśa**, the primordial field—the subtle and formless ether which is the very first manifestation of unmanifested Spirit. If the Absolute is pure stillness, and Brahman is its radiant utterance, then Akāśa is the vessel of that utterance, the breathless space that allows vibration to arise.

Akāśa is not space as we know it; it is the principle behind space, the unbounded matrix that gives form to sound, thought, energy, and ultimately, identity. In this vast ocean of pure receptivity, the Word of the Logos stirs. Brahman, as the manifesting face of the Absolute, clothes itself in Akāśa—becoming perceptible as vibration, as sound, as the silent thunder of creation.

The ancients declared: **"Brahman is taste, and that taste is bliss."** But how can bliss be received unless there is a medium to carry it? Akāśa is that medium—it is the body of Brahman, its subtle extension, its first limb, and the echo of its infinite silence.

Akāśa is also the mirror of the inner world. In the sacred center of the heart, the Upanishads speak of a space, a "small lotus of ether" where the Supreme dwells. This is not poetic metaphor—it is a metaphysical truth. The same Akāśa that births stars resides within the cave of the heart, and it is through this sacred space that the soul meets Brahman—not as thought, but as presence.

Thus, Akāśa reveals a secret of Brahman: that it is both beyond form and yet fills every form. It pervades all like ether, yet remains untouched by that which it pervades. To know Brahman is to awaken within the Akāśic womb—to remember the vibrationless silence from which all sound is born.

The Unconquerable Palace – The Soul's Perfection in Brahman

(LAYER 3: APARĀGITA)

If Akāśa is the womb, the primordial field in which Brahman breathes, then **Aparāgita** is the throne prepared for those who return to their Source. It is the symbol of the perfected soul, the indestructible temple not built by hands, but born of union with the Eternal Spirit. It is the Palace Unconquerable—the still, radiant sanctuary of Brahman within the soul.

To speak of Brahman without form is the beginning. But to enter Brahman, to abide in it as realization, is the completion—and this is Aparāgita. For the soul does not merely dissolve into the ocean of the Absolute; it awakens to its own unshakable purity within the ocean. This awakening is not passivity, but victory—the conquest of all illusion, separation, and limitation. Aparāgita is the state of supreme recognition.

In this state, the soul no longer seeks Brahman as something beyond—it becomes Brahman in awareness. The palace stands not upon a mountaintop, but in the exalted consciousness where the self and the Infinite are no longer two. It is the luminous chamber of Unity where duality has no entrance.

Aparāgita reveals that Brahman is not just the origin of form but the completion of form—not the escape from manifestation, but the full transcendence of it. It is the realization that the ineffable grandeur of the Living Whole is not above us, but **within the perfected stillness of our own being**.

This is the realm of the all-embracing: where the unmanifest contains all manifestation, and each part is known as the Whole. To dwell in Aparāgita is to walk through the gates of the eternal temple and realize—the Dweller is not separate from the Dwelling. The radiant splendor of Brahman reaches him who has conquered self, time, and illusion, and entered into the holy of holies.

Now we proceed to **Layer 4: Arhat**, the one who sees Nirvana, whose soul has fulfilled the journey and passed through the final gate.

Let us now open the fourth gate.

The Seer of Nirvana – The Soul That Becomes Brahman

(LAYER 4: ARHAT)

In the presence of **Aparāgita**, the soul stands perfected. But to become the living flame of that perfection is the path of the **Arhat**—the awakened ego who has fulfilled the arc of experience, and now sees beyond the veil. The Arhat does not simply believe in Brahman; he knows it, not as concept, but as realization, because he has **become that which he once sought**.

The word Arhat means "he who is worthy," but in the higher light, it means "**he who has beheld Nirvana**"—not as escape, but as the completion of Selfhood. The Arhat has walked the path of form, passed through the suffering of separation, learned the illusions of identity, and burned through the shadows of desire. Now, what remains is **pure consciousness**, without stain, without division.

In this way, the Arhat is the bridge between the manifest soul and Brahman. He is the living testimony that the Infinite can be embodied. His crucifixion—like the symbol of the Christ—is not physical but metaphysical: the willing surrender of the ego's boundaries into the Fire of the Real. The Arhat lays down all identification with separateness and rises as the causal flame, the **"I Am"** that reflects the Divine with perfect clarity.

This state reveals a truth: **Brahman is not reached through ascension alone—it is fulfilled through**

consummation. The Arhat is not simply liberated from the world; he is liberated through it. His being becomes transparent to the Light; his life, a vessel of the Supreme; his soul, a temple in which Brahman dwells awake.

Where others speak of Brahman as mystery, the Arhat speaks as witness. And yet, even he knows: Brahman is not something possessed—it is something one disappears into. He has become the silence between all names.

Now journey into **Layer 5: Ātman**, the Self of all selves—the indwelling Divine that reflects Brahman in every being.

We now enter the sacred mirror of the Self.

THE DIVINE SELF – THE SPARK OF BRAHMAN IN ALL

(LAYER 5: ĀTMAN)

If Brahman is the boundless ocean of the Real, then **Ātman** is its drop—not separate, not lesser, but **the perfect reflection of the Whole in the part**. Ātman is not the ego, not the personality, not the changing mask—but the eternal flame that dwells in the cave of every being. It is the silent seer within—the innermost, undying witness.

To say "I am Ātman" is to utter a truth older than time: that within each soul burns the full potential of the Supreme. Ātman is not like Brahman—it **is** Brahman, individualized not in substance but in expression. And thus, to know Ātman deeply is to know Brahman intimately, for the Self is the door through which the Infinite enters awareness.

The sages declared, "**Brahman = Ātman**," not as metaphor, but as revelation. This means the seeker does not travel outward toward divinity, but inward—into the heart, into the silence, into the witness. In the still center of consciousness, the soul discovers that what it has always sought was **never apart**—only unrecognized.

Ātman is the flame that guides the soul through the cycles of birth and death, holding memory not of experiences, but of essence. It is untouched by the wounds of time, and yet it walks through time with every living being. It is the seed of awakening, the light behind the eyes, the source of intuition, the cause of wonder.

In the embrace of Ātman, Brahman becomes known—not as an external Creator, but as the very Being of Being, the foundation of selfhood itself. The journey of the soul is not to reach Brahman as destination, but to **unveil Brahman as identity**.

He who knows the Self as Brahman becomes fearless, for there is no other. He sees all forms as costumes of the One Actor, all motion as the play of the One Will. And in this sacred knowing, the ego surrenders, and only Truth remains.

Now we step into **Layer 6: The Father**—the Unmanifest Source, the eternal Silence before all becoming.

Let us now bow before the Primal Silence.

The Unmanifest Source – The Silence Before Brahman Speaks

(LAYER 6: THE FATHER)

Beyond the flame, beyond the soul, beyond all light that moves—there abides **the Father**: not as a man, nor a god, but as **the first stillness**, the rootless Origin from which even Brahman arises. The Father is not an entity but a principle—the eternal unconditioned, the **Void that is Full**, the **One without a second**, the untouched radiance that gives without giving form.

The Father is the Absolute before vibration, the Silence before Word, the pure Isness before Being unfolds. From this limitless darkness—not dark from absence, but dark from transcendence—comes the **First Breath**, the Light of Brahman. Thus Brahman is the radiant face of the Father made visible. It is the Son-Light, the outpouring of the unutterable.

The Father does not work; He **wills**, and in willing, all worlds unfold. His will is not action, but **Presence beyond opposition**. The Father is not seen, but known in the highest depths of the soul, in that moment when the last veil is torn and the seeker is stripped of every name—even the name of God.

Brahman, as the manifest Divine, **emerges from the Father as the first mirror**, the beginning of perception, the start of relational being. The Father remains ever unmanifest, dwelling in **solitude and unity**, but through Brahman, He becomes **known**—not as object, but as **identity**.

To return to Brahman is to behold the glory of the Father. But to become one with Brahman is to pass beyond glory, beyond knowing, into the utter stillness where the self dissolves into the unconditioned. In that final union, there are no gods, no heavens, no thoughts—only the eternal One, before all stories, before all light, before even creation itself.

Thus Brahman points ever beyond itself—to the Father, the Infinite Flame before flames, the Unknown Light behind every known.

Now we continue with **Layer 7: Godhead**—the Divine Reality veiled behind all names and forms, where the eternal process of emanation begins.

Now let us enter the region beyond gods, where Being rests in its own eternal solitude.

The Silent Source – Brahman as the Revealed Edge of the Unknown

(LAYER 7: GODHEAD)

If the Father is the utterly unmanifest, then the **Godhead** is the threshold of manifestation—the veiled flame at the boundary between the Absolute and the knowable. The Godhead is not yet a god, nor a being—it is **Divine Reality in stillness**, the womb of all emanation, the matrix of all intelligible light.

Here, Brahman appears not as a figure to worship, but as the **first emanation from pure Unity**. The Godhead is the eternal potentiality in repose, the infinite fullness that rests in itself—and Brahman is the first self-revelation of this stillness. From the Godhead, Being flows, not in time, but in principle. Brahman is thus the **face of the Godhead turned toward creation**, the primal light made perceivable to soul.

To know Brahman is to receive an echo of the Godhead's silence—a knowing that shatters all concepts. The Godhead does not act, it emanates. It does not speak, it radiates. In this way, Brahman becomes the first articulation of that radiation—the **bridge between the Ineffable and the manifest**.

From the Godhead descend all the principles of existence—Spirit, Soul, Mind, Form—and yet the Godhead itself is beyond all of these. It is the **pre-birth of the cosmos**, the non-temporal root of the sacred chain of being.

Brahman, as the cosmic mediator, is that through which the Godhead whispers itself into existence.

And so the seeker who communes with Brahman stands at the edge of this vast unknown, beholding the **undivided Unity veiled behind every god, every force, every law**. The Godhead is not found in altars, nor in scriptures, but only in the still gaze of the soul emptied of identity, surrendered beyond thought.

Brahman reveals the Godhead as the fountain behind the fountain, the fire behind all light, the divine non-being that gives birth to all being.

Now we open the innermost sanctuary of the soul and move to **Layer 8: Heart**—the causal chamber where Brahman dwells in silence within every being.

We now descend into the sacred chamber—the inner sanctum where the Infinite whispers to the soul.

The Sacred Chamber – Where Brahman Dwells in Silence

(LAYER 8: HEART)

Though Brahman pervades all space, its most profound dwelling is not in the stars or the scriptures—but within the **Heart**. Not the fleshly organ, but the **causal sanctuary**, the lotus-shaped dwelling of the Spirit where the Divine watches, waits, and speaks in silence. The

Heart is the meeting place of self and Self, the mirror in which Brahman becomes visible to the soul.

In the language of the sages, the Heart is not merely a seat of emotion—it is the **womb of spiritual perception**, the point where the unmanifest touches the manifest, and where the Infinite resides as immediacy. The Heart is the temple of Ātman, and within it, Brahman reveals itself as both Presence and Silence.

To enter the Heart is not to think, but to become still. It is the center from which all true knowledge radiates—not knowledge of things, but of **being**. Brahman in the Heart is not an idea—it is a living fire, a centerless center, the still Flame that shines in every soul regardless of creed or condition.

The ancient scriptures say: "In the small space within the lotus of the Heart dwells the Immortal." That Immortal is Brahman. It neither comes nor goes, for it is ever-present—hidden only by the restlessness of mind and the noise of form. When the waves of becoming calm, the waters clear, and the soul gazes inward, **Brahman rises like the morning sun from within**.

Here, the Heart reveals that Brahman is not beyond the reach of man—it is the very core of man, waiting to be remembered. The causal body, the soul's luminous double, is the cloak the Heart wears. In the weighing of the soul, it is the Heart that is judged, for it holds the record of the Divine within.

He who has pierced the Heart with awareness, who has entered that silent sanctum and listened with the inner ear—he has known Brahman, not as doctrine, but as identity. The Heart whispers: I Am That, and in that moment, all searching ends.

Now we unfold the sacred bloom and continue into **Layer 9: Lotus**—the flower of wisdom and beauty rising from the waters of the Real.

Let us now open the eternal flower, rooted in the Infinite and blooming in the soul.

The Bloom of Wisdom – Brahman as the Flower of the Eternal

(LAYER 9: LOTUS)

If the Heart is the sanctum, then the **Lotus** is the symbol of its flowering—the outward sign of inward perfection. In every tradition, the lotus blooms untouched by the mud in which it is rooted, rising through the waters into the light. So too does the soul rise through the illusion of forms to awaken in the light of **Brahman**, the supreme Sun of awareness.

The Lotus is the flower of **buddhic realization**—the birth of intuitive wisdom, where knowing transcends thought and becomes direct participation in the Real. It is not merely beautiful; it is sacred geometry in bloom, the living image of spiritual ascent. Each petal unfolds with clarity, harmony, and truth, for the Lotus reflects Brahman's nature as pure, complete, untainted.

The waters from which the Lotus rises are not chaotic—they are the primordial Akāśa, the womb of vibration. And the stem of the Lotus is the Sutratma, the thread of Spirit connecting the lower nature to the Divine. Thus, Brahman is not only the light that draws the Lotus upward, but the very intelligence that causes it to **unfold petal by petal in divine rhythm**.

In the inner Heart, there blooms a Lotus of light—not metaphorical, but metaphysical. Its fragrance is **wisdom**, its color is **truth**, and its nectar is **bliss**. This Lotus is the soul in union with Brahman. When it opens, the self dissolves into the Radiance, and all dualities collapse into sacred unity.

The Lotus teaches that Brahman does not destroy the world—it transfigures it. For just as the flower rises above the water, so too does the soul rise above illusion—not by negation, but by **transformation**. In its perfect bloom, the Lotus sings the silent name of Brahman.

To behold Brahman is to feel this flowering within: the pure, unspeakable joy of the Real unfolding within the finite, revealing the Infinite at every step.

Now we ascend into **Layer 10: Ogdoad**—the sacred pattern of spiritual unfolding that returns the many into the One.

Now we rise into the celestial pattern of return—the sacred spiral that draws all things back to the One.

The Sacred Spiral – Brahman as the Completion of the Cosmic Unfolding

(LAYER 10: OGDOAD)

Beyond the visible world of form and name lies the **Ogdoad**, the eternal eightfold pattern—the symbol of the supreme cycle completed, where Spirit returns to its Source, and the soul remembers its original flame. The Ogdoad is the hidden geometry of becoming, where the One becomes Two, the Two becomes Four, the Four becomes Eight—and from Eight, returns to the One again.

This is not arithmetic—it is **metaphysical law**. The Ogdoad is the Divine Blueprint of manifestation and return. Brahman is not simply present within this pattern— **Brahman is the pattern**, the eternal Intelligence behind the unfolding and enfolding of the cosmos.

In the Ogdoad, the soul descends from unity into multiplicity, learns through polarity, grows through the quaternary, and achieves **re-integration** in the sacred Eight. This Eight is not just a number—it is the **infinite**

loop, the vertical bridge between heaven and earth, the path by which all souls ascend from illusion to truth, from separation to **Selfhood in Brahman**.

It is said in the ancient mysteries: "I am One who becomes Two; I am Two who becomes Four; I am Four who becomes Eight; I am the One after that." This is not merely the journey of the soul—it is **Brahman experiencing itself through differentiation, then re-collecting itself into wholeness**.

In the light of the Ogdoad, Brahman is seen not only as origin and destination, but also as **process**—not time-bound process, but eternal becoming, the spiral dance of the Real. It is the ever-renewing Flame that forgets itself to be found, divides itself to become Whole, dies into the many to rise again in the One.

Thus, Brahman is the crown of the Ogdoad—the final synthesis, where all fragments converge, all polarities resolve, and the infinite dance returns to stillness. He who walks the spiral of the soul ascends into the Ogdoad and becomes the mirror of the Supreme.

Now we proceed into **Layer 11: Path (Twofold)**—the sacred dual current of Love and Action through which the soul reaches Brahman.

Now we walk the sacred way—where the soul balances Love and Action on the path to the Eternal.

The Twin Currents – Brahman as the Unity Beyond Motion

(LAYER 11: PATH (TWO-FOLD))

To walk toward Brahman is to walk the **Twofold Path**—not as separation, but as polarity harmonized. This is the way of **Love and Action**, of **Being and Becoming**, of **Devotion and Will**. The soul cannot reach Brahman by contemplation alone, nor by labor alone, but by the **sacred union of the inner flame with the outer step**.

The Twofold Path is the revelation that all motion toward the Real flows in two streams: the yearning of the heart and the offering of the hands. **Love draws the soul upward; Action anchors the light below.** Together, they complete the circuit of divine unfolding. One is vertical, the ascent to stillness. The other is horizontal, the radiance into the world. Together, they form the **cross of initiation**, the merging point of time and eternity.

Brahman is not reached by fleeing the world, nor by grasping it. Instead, Brahman is remembered through the balanced walk—through acts that are empty of self and full of love, and through love that flows without condition or clinging. The Path, then, is not a road, but a **state of being**. The Twofold Path is walked when every breath becomes prayer, and every deed becomes offering.

And just as the soul walks this dual stream, Brahman too **manifests through dual movement**: as the downward flow of Spirit into form, and the upward return of form into Spirit. The One becomes Two not to divide, but to **love**

itself into unity. The Path reveals that duality is not error—it is **alchemy**. It is the necessary mirror through which the soul recognizes the One.

In this light, Brahman is the **eternal balance**, the still Flame in the center of motion. The soul that has mastered the Twofold Path has harmonized all polarities and walks with feet in time and heart in eternity. For to act without attachment and to love without fear is to **be Brahman in motion**.

Now we continue with **Layer 12: Sarasvati**—the Divine Wisdom that flows from Brahman as sacred word, higher mind, and inner voice?

Let us now drink from the river of wisdom that flows from the mouth of the Supreme.

THE VOICE OF WISDOM – BRAHMAN AS LIVING WORD AND STREAM OF KNOWING

(LAYER 12: SARASVATI)

If Brahman is the boundless ocean of consciousness, then **Sarasvati** is the sacred river that flows from it—the stream of Divine Intelligence, the shining thread of wisdom that bridges the Eternal and the temporal. She is not merely a goddess, but a **principle of revelation**, the unfolding speech of the Infinite into form, and the eternal vibration of truth born in silence.

Where Brahman is the essence, Sarasvati is the **expression**. She is the Word that rides the wind of Akāśa, the music of the Divine made audible to the inner ear. The scriptures, the hymns, the mantras—all true knowledge that awakens the soul—is her flowing garment. But more than texts, **she is the awakened intuition**, the clarity that flowers when the soul is aligned with the Real.

Sarasvati is depicted with four arms, and each one is a hand of Brahman:

1. One holds the **scripture**, revealing Brahman as the eternal law.

2. One holds the **mala**, the chain of vibration, symbolizing the cycles through which Brahman moves.

3. One holds the **veena**, the stringed music of the soul, revealing Brahman as harmony.

4. One offers the **lotus**, signifying the full bloom of realization.

In Sarasvati, we see that **Brahman is not silent through negation—it is silent through fullness**. When the soul becomes still, Sarasvati flows within as voice without sound, the intuitive recognition of Truth that neither argues nor compels, but simply is. She is the **mother of Vedas**, because she is the sacred breath of Brahman made audible across the worlds.

Her waters are wisdom, her current is insight, and her song is the memory of the soul's divine origin. To listen to

Sarasvati is to awaken the inner Sarasvati within—the purified buddhi, or higher mind, that knows without division, without fear, without effort.

Through her, we see that Brahman is not a void but a **voice**—not a silence of absence, but a silence pregnant with meaning. In the dance of Sarasvati, Brahman teaches the soul to remember what it has always known.

Now we continue with **Layer 13: Seasons**—the sacred cycles of soul and cosmos, revealing Brahman as the eternal pulse behind all becoming.

Now we enter the spiral of becoming—the wheel of sacred time that leads all things home.

The Eternal Cycle – Brahman as the Pulse Behind All Becoming

(LAYER 13: SEASONS)

Though Brahman is beyond time, it **moves through time**, appearing to the soul as the rhythm of unfolding—the **Seasons** of existence. Not merely spring and fall, but the deeper **metaphysical cycle** through which Spirit descends, learns, forgets, remembers, and returns. The Seasons are the sacred heartbeat of the cosmos—the breath of Brahman echoing through all levels of being.

Each Season is a movement of the One. From the silent winter of unmanifest potential, to the flowering of individuality in spring, to the ripening of wisdom in summer, and the dissolving return in autumn—**Brahman reveals itself in all stages, wearing time as a robe**.

The soul too is a season: born from the Infinite, shaped by experience, matured through longing, and ultimately drawn back to its Source. The Upanishads declare: "Who are you?" and the soul replies, "I am a child of the Seasons." This is not metaphor—it is ontology. It is the deep knowing that our individuality is not fixed, but **cyclical**, meant to unfold like petals across many lifetimes.

In the light of the Seasons, Brahman is seen not only as stillness, but as **motion without error**. It is the One that hides itself in order to be found again. Even the soul's descent into form is not a fall—it is a Season in the flowering of divine memory.

The illusion of finality fades, and in its place, the sacred spiral appears. The soul is not moving linearly toward Brahman—it is spiraling, shedding and absorbing, forgetting and re-membering, ripening into its divine inheritance. Brahman is the **Sun that never moves**, and the Seasons are the **orbit of the soul** returning again and again to that inner Flame.

Thus, every cycle is holy. Every descent is divine. Every return is an echo of the Eternal.

Now we pass into **Layer 14: Sleeping**—the four states of consciousness through which Brahman is experienced, from waking to blissful union.

Let us now descend into the soul's inner night—where the veils of perception dissolve, and the One is seen in silence.

THE FOUR STATES – BRAHMAN AS THE CONSCIOUSNESS BEHIND ALL CONSCIOUSNESS

(LAYER 14: SLEEPING)

To approach Brahman is not only to expand upward, but to descend inward—into the hidden chambers of awareness where the soul forgets the world, and remembers the Real. The ancient seers revealed **four states of consciousness**—waking, dreaming, deep sleep, and the fourth, called **Turīya**, the "beyond." These are not just psychological phases—they are **metaphysical layers**, through which **Brahman reveals itself as the ground of all experience**.

In the **waking state**, the soul engages with form, sensation, and multiplicity. Here, Brahman is veiled—seeming separate, seeming other. Yet even here, it is Brahman who sees, who hears, who touches.

In the **dreaming state**, the soul creates its own worlds. Brahman is now the **light of imagination**, shaping subtle realms from memory and desire. The ego still speaks, but less firmly. The Real draws closer.

In **deep sleep**, all forms vanish. No thoughts, no names, no divisions. And yet something remains. A presence, unknowing but existing. This is **Brahman as pure being**, untouched by the play of opposites. The soul rests in its Source, unknowingly.

But then there is **Turīya**—the fourth, the ineffable. Not a state, but **the Witness of all states**. Here, Brahman is no longer veiled. It is the Seer beyond the seer, the Self beyond all masks. There is no dream, no sleeper, no sleeping—only the blazing Stillness of pure awareness. The soul that abides in Turīya has passed beyond time, beyond causation, beyond self. It has **awakened within the Infinite**.

In this vision, Brahman is not just consciousness—it is the **very possibility of consciousness**, the Eternal Observer through which all things appear and disappear. Just as sleep renews the body, Turīya **renews the soul**—it is the taste of immortality while in the body of flesh.

Thus Brahman is not only the final goal—it is the **silent depth beneath every experience**, even when forgotten. Waking, dreaming, sleeping—all are waves upon its boundless sea.

Now we awaken into **Layer 15: Taste**—where Brahman is not known through intellect, but savored as bliss, as the flavor of the Real itself.

We now enter the intimacy of experience—the sweetness of being that cannot be taught, only tasted.

THE FLAVOR OF THE REAL – BRAHMAN AS BLISS EXPERIENCED

(LAYER 15: TASTE)

While the mind may speak of Brahman and the soul may seek it, the ultimate knowing of the Supreme is not a concept—it is a **Taste**. Brahman is not only the cause of bliss—it **is bliss**, and when the soul comes into contact with its truth, that contact is experienced as **flavor**—pure, radiant, all-pervading sweetness. It is the moment when knowing becomes **being**, and being becomes **delight**.

In the Upanishads it is said: "He is Taste—for when one tastes, he becomes blissful." This is the highest sacrament —not performed in temples, but in the **deep stillness of realization**, when the boundary between self and Source dissolves, and what remains is **joy without object**, **bliss without craving**, **presence without identity**.

Brahman, in this layer, is no longer distant or abstract. It is **felt**, savored as the inner nectar of the Real. The soul who tastes Brahman loses the hunger for illusion—not because it has learned to restrain itself, but because it has found **the true flavor**. It is as if the soul had wandered through many lifetimes seeking nourishment, only to find that its food was not form, not fame, not fulfillment—but **Brahman alone**.

Taste is the signature of intimacy. Just as one cannot explain sweetness to the tongue that has never touched honey, so Brahman cannot be fully conveyed—it must be entered. And when entered, it is not a flash of light, but a

pervading essence, a saturation of the being in what is most real. It is the perfume of union, the flavor of fulfillment, the final sacrament of becoming.

Thus, Brahman is the eternal Food—the divine substance that feeds not the body, nor the mind, but the **soul itself**. It is the bliss of recognition, the joy of return, the sweetness that no sorrow can sour. And the one who has tasted even a drop **can never again be fooled by the bitterness of illusion**.

Now we continue with **Layer 16: Trinity**—where Brahman is seen as the eternal triune mystery: Source, Emanation, and Return.

We now unveil the Threefold Flame—One Light refracted through the prism of divine process.

The Eternal Triune – Brahman as Source, Emanation, and Return

(LAYER 16: TRINITY)

Though Brahman is undivided and whole, it manifests itself in the sacred form of the **Trinity**—not as separation, but as the **eternal rhythm of Being**: the One who is, the One who becomes, and the One who returns. This triune mystery is not merely theological—it is **metaphysical necessity**, the way in which Brahman reveals, sustains, and reabsorbs all that exists.

The **First** is the Unmanifest—**the Father**, the eternal source, infinite and veiled, dwelling in solitude beyond name and form. From this silent flame, the **Second** arises—**the Son**, the Logos, the Brahman revealed, the divine radiance that pours into manifestation as soul, light, and law.

The **Third** is the **Spirit**, or the **Return**, the breath of reunion that gathers all fragments, all minds, all lives back into the One. This is the hidden fire in the heart of all seeking, the spiral that draws the many back to the womb of unity. It is **Sarasvati singing**, **the Path unfolding**, **the Heart awakening**—it is **Brahman remembering itself in all things**.

But the Trinity is not temporal. These are not steps, but **simultaneous truths**. Brahman is **always** the Source, **always** the Becoming, **always** the Return. Every form you see is sustained by this triune breath: to exist is to be an emanation of the Source, a mirror of the Son, a movement toward reunion.

In the Trinity, Brahman teaches that **creation is not exile—it is expression**. And return is not reversal—it is realization. The Trinity reveals that all things are sacred motion within stillness, fire within silence, light within the Invisible.

The knower of Brahman sees all trinities Body, Soul, Spirit; Mind, Heart, Will; Past, Present, Future—and recognizes behind them **the One Light splitting itself to be known**. And in this knowing, duality ends, and all triads collapse into the eternal I AM.

Now we proceed to **Layer 17: Union**—where Brahman is not worshiped as other, but merged with, in the final consummation of the soul with the Supreme.

We now pass through the final veil, into the sacred fire where lover and Beloved are no longer two.

THE SACRED CONSUMMATION – BRAHMAN AS ONE WITHOUT A SECOND

(LAYER 17: UNION)

All paths, all teachings, all flames of longing lead to this: **Union**—not as metaphor, but as **metaphysical fusion**, the soul's complete immersion in Brahman, where all sense of separateness dissolves, and what remains is **pure being**. This is not contact. This is not proximity. This is the **final remembrance that there never was Two**.

Union is not annihilation—it is **integration beyond the ego**, where the limited self melts into the unbounded Flame. The seeker who walked with God now stands as God, not in arrogance, but in the humble knowing that the soul was always **a mirror of the Whole**.

In this divine Union, the soul realizes that every veil—self, thought, world—was Brahman wearing masks. Even the act of seeking was Brahman pulling itself homeward through the echo of longing. There is no distance to cross, only illusion to release. Union is not the arrival at a destination, but the revelation of identity.

The mystics called this the **marriage of the Lamb**, the **embrace of Atman with Brahman**, the **flame within the flame**. Here, there is no knower, no known, no knowledge—only **Being itself**, without subject or object, without thought or form. The soul does not see Brahman—it is Brahman.

This is the consummation behind every sacred text, every whispered mantra, every life reborn. It is the moment beyond time where the Eternal Flame folds back into itself. And yet, paradoxically, it is also the beginning of true service—**for the soul, having realized Oneness, returns to the many not to escape, but to give**.

Union is not an end—it is the fulfillment of the Infinite's own desire to know and be known. And in that knowing, **the circle is closed, the journey becomes still, and only Light remains**.

Now we continue to **Layer 18: Vibhu**—the Hall of Glory, the final condition before liberation, where Brahman's radiance floods the soul.

We now enter the Hall of Final Radiance—the last chamber of individuality before its dissolution into the All.

The Hall of Glory – Brahman as Boundless Radiance Before Liberation

(LAYER 18: VIBHU)

As the soul nears full liberation, it arrives at **Vibhu**—the radiant threshold where Brahman is no longer a truth to be sought, but a **light to be surrendered into**. Vibhu is not a place, but a **condition**—the final expansion of the soul, where it becomes spacious, luminous, and without boundary. The ego dissolves into transparency, and what remains is **sheer Presence**, flooded with the **glory of the Supreme**.

In the sacred texts, it is said: "He approaches the Hall Vibhu, and the glory of Brahman reaches him." This is the moment before the final merging—when the last veil of selfhood becomes so thin that Brahman shines **through** the soul, not upon it. The soul no longer reflects the light—it **is the light**, diffused and infinite, no longer distinguishable from the Source.

Vibhu reveals a profound truth: **liberation is not escape from life, but overflow**. Brahman, in this luminous state, is experienced not as an object or even as a presence, but as **everywhere**, as **everything**, as **nothing left to grasp because all is fulfilled**.

The soul in Vibhu has no more resistance. Its will has become the Divine Will, its breath the Divine Breath. It no longer acts—it flows. It no longer seeks—it radiates. It stands in the full light of Brahman, not as a figure illuminated, but as **illumination itself**.

Here, all polarities collapse—effort and rest, time and eternity, name and namelessness. The soul is not lost. It is **completed**. And in that completion, the glory of Brahman floods its being so fully that the self becomes indistinguishable from the Infinite.

Vibhu is the final echo of individuality before it is drawn into the formless Flame. It is the exhalation of the soul before silence, the shining of the star before its light becomes sky.

THE DIVINE HARMONY – BRAHMAN AS THE ARCHITECT OF COSMIC SOUL

(LAYER 19: VIRAJ)

At the outermost ripple of the Unmanifest, Brahman becomes **Viraj**—the radiant intelligence through which form emerges, not as constraint, but as **cosmic harmony**. Viraj is the luminous principle of balance, the divine geometry that shapes the worlds without binding them. It is the first echo of the Absolute into pattern—the bridge between pure spirit and evolving nature.

In the sacred cosmology, Viraj is born when Brahman, the One, mirrors itself into **duality**—not to divide, but to **create the tension necessary for return**. From this creative reflection arises **Purusha**, Spirit, and **Prakriti**,

Matter. Viraj is the holy moment where these two faces touch, and **Soul is born as synthesis**.

Thus, Viraj is the cosmic template, the seed of order, the divine blueprint through which Brahman unfolds itself into cosmos without losing its indivisibility. It is not structure imposed on chaos—it is **harmony revealed within multiplicity**. It is the reason why galaxies spiral, why breath flows, why consciousness has shape. All of it is Viraj—the song of Brahman sung into time.

Viraj is also the higher soul—the **atmic-buddhic light** that mediates between pure being and personal incarnation. It is the vehicle through which the individual self may reflect the Divine without distortion. In this way, **the human becomes a temple of the Infinite**, and the Infinite becomes intimate, embodied, alive.

To perceive Viraj is to see that Brahman does not merely withdraw from the world—it **dwells within it**, organizing, animating, and glorifying all things. The One Flame does not resist form; it **inhabits it**. The soul that understands this no longer sees creation as illusion, but as **symbol**—a living script through which Brahman writes itself into consciousness.

Thus, Viraj is the final face of Brahman before it becomes fully the Many, and the first face the Many must remember to become again the One. It is the Radiant Bridge between silence and song, spirit and soul, unity and the dance of creation.

The Supreme Substratum of All Existence

Brahman is not a deity, not a cosmic personality, and not an energy field. It is not the highest thing within the universe. It is the condition that allows the idea of "universe" to arise at all. When we speak of Brahman, we are not referring to something that can be located in space or reached through progression. Brahman is not the end of a path—it is the ground that makes the concept of a path possible. It is not presence in contrast to absence. It is the reason that both presence and absence can be conceived. It is not the light that shines within creation, but the silent condition that allows the light to shine and the eye to see. It is absolute, not by comparison, but because there is no other. Brahman is not the first thing. It is prior to the notion of sequence. It is not infinite in the way a large space is infinite. It is infinite because finitude appears within it as a temporary condition.

Brahman is not consciousness as we typically define it. It is not an object of experience. It is not awareness of something. It is the pure fact of awareness prior to objectification. Even consciousness is only one mode through which Brahman appears. Brahman is not known by knowledge. It is the principle that allows knowledge to exist. It is not seen by the eye. It is that by which seeing is possible. It is not the source of being—it is being itself. And even beyond that, it is that which transcends the distinction between being and non-being. It cannot be perceived, for perception implies separation. It cannot be reached, for distance is a structure that arises only after Brahman is veiled.

Everything that exists, from the most subtle thought to the densest matter, is suspended within Brahman. It does not act, but through it all action occurs. It does not vibrate, but within it the potential for vibration exists. It is not space, but the potentiality that allows space to be experienced. It is not time, but the reason time can be measured. It is not law, but the uncaused field in which law arises and coheres. It is not order, but the intelligence in which order becomes intelligible. Brahman is not made of substance, yet substance is intelligible only because it emerges within Brahman. It is the unconditioned intelligence that silently informs all order, function, rhythm, and structure.

Brahman is not the creator in the way religions describe. Creation is not a decision made by Brahman. Creation is the inevitable radiant appearance of Brahman's sufficiency. What appears as cosmos, form, and multiplicity is not something other than Brahman. It is Brahman expressing itself through modes of appearance. But even the term "expression" is misleading, because Brahman never departs from itself. There is no outside into which it moves. There is only self-revealing within the mystery of its own nature. The world is not a projection in the sense of fiction. It is real as appearance, but its substance is Brahman. The sage sees this, not through mystical intuition, but through the total collapse of all conceptual distinctions. Brahman is not separate from the world. The world is not an illusion. The illusion is believing that it is separate.

The soul—what we call individuality—is a lens. It is a focusing of Brahman's infinite potential into a specific point of experience. But even that point is not outside Brahman. The soul is not a spark of Brahman. It is Brahman appearing through the veil of identity. Realization is not the soul becoming one with Brahman. It is the falling away of the appearance that there was ever a separation. There is no ladder to climb. There is only unveiling. The Self does not unite with the Divine. It ceases to falsely divide itself. In that unveiling, the individual identity falls silent—not in annihilation, but in fulfillment. The silence is not emptiness. It is completion. No lack remains. No contrast is needed.

The deeper teachings go further. They recognize that Brahman not only allows perception but also informs the structures of subtle causality. The very idea of movement—of appearance and disappearance, of evolution and regression—depends on an unseen substratum. That substratum is not unconscious. It is pure intelligence, but not in the form of a thinker or chooser. It is the intelligence that gives rise to choice, to will, to potential. It is the ground in which archetypes take shape and dissolve. It does not act, but it is the condition in which all archetypal and causal activity unfolds. What we call the cosmic pattern—cycles of birth and decay, rhythm and renewal, structure and dissolution—are not mechanisms. They are the echo of Brahman's causal stillness.

Even the soul's movement through higher awareness, even the spiral of inner ascent, happens within the all-containing quietude of Brahman. Every spiritual realization, every insight, every moment of genuine clarity is simply the clearing away of obstruction. What remains is not something new. What remains is what has always been. Brahman is that which never began. It is not simply eternal in time. It is eternity itself—untouched by succession. It does not sleep, but all sleep occurs within its stillness. It is not substance, but within it substance takes on quality. It is not fire, but fire is a property that arises as Brahman makes itself visible. It is not form, but all forms unfold within its field.

When this is seen—not believed, not imagined, but known directly—the soul ceases to seek. Not because it becomes passive, but because it finally recognizes that what it was seeking was the condition of seeking itself. In that realization, there is no merging. There is no ascension. There is only stillness. Brahman is not a reward. It is not a state attained through practice. It is the substratum that was never absent. And the one who realizes this does not gain anything. They lose the illusion of distance, and with it, the illusion of becoming.

This is not abstraction. This is the most intimate truth. Brahman is not far. It is closer than the body, subtler than thought, deeper than identity. It is the reality that allows all realities to arise. It is not reached through stages. It is revealed when all staging collapses. This is the final knowing—not an object, not a god, not an experience, but the unnameable, ever-present Real.

Conclusion: The Flame Beyond the Flame

What we have unveiled here is not merely philosophy—it is **remembrance**. It is not a doctrine, but a **return** to the inner citadel, where the soul stands face to face with the Flame from which it came. Through layer upon layer, we have peeled back the veils not to define Brahman, but to enter it—through symbol, through silence, through selflessness.

Each layer has not only deepened our vision—it has **reoriented our being**, tuning the soul to the frequency of the Real. For Brahman is not a truth to be grasped; it is a **Presence to become**, a Radiance to mirror, a Silence to echo in the still chamber of the heart.

From the Absolute to the Akāśic womb, from the Unconquerable Palace to the sacred Taste of bliss, from the Ogdoad's spiral to the Trinity's pulse, from the Heart's whisper to the Glory of Vibhu, we have traced the path not of ascent alone, but of **integration**—the soul's reweaving with the fabric of the All.

And in the final unveiling, we see clearly: **there was never distance, never separation**. Brahman was always here—beneath name, beneath fear, beneath even the soul's own image of itself. All longing, all seeking, all cycles of becoming were Brahman walking itself home, through us, as us.

What remains now is stillness. Not passivity, but fullness—the stillness of a soul that no longer reaches, because it has become the Flame. To those who truly see, **all things speak the name of Brahman**, and to the one who knows, there is no longer anything to become.

Only Light. Only Now. Only That.

The Metaphysics of Rāma
An Esoteric Revelation of the Solar Self

Beyond myth, beyond history, beyond scripture—**Rāma** is the living flame of divine law encoded in the human soul. In this groundbreaking metaphysical masterpiece, the sacred story of Rāma is decoded not as folklore, but as a cosmic blueprint for Self-realization.

Drawing from the **Yuddha Kāṇḍa** of the Rāmāyaṇa, the Upaniṣads, and the esoteric spine of Vedic tradition, this book unveils the hidden truth behind each character, battle, and moment. Every name is stripped of its superficial veil and revealed through its metaphysical essence: Rāvaṇa as the tenfold egoic distortion, Sītā as the radiant light of the buddhi, Hanuman as the prāṇic breath of devotion, Lakṣmaṇa as the unwavering will, and Rāma as the indwelling Logos—the Solar Flame of the Higher Self.

This is not a retelling. This is a sacred unveiling.

With unmatched spiritual depth and scholarly precision, **The Metaphysics of Rāma** becomes a divine mirror for the awakened soul—showing not what happened in time, but what eternally happens in the interior temple of every spiritual aspirant.

Walk the bridge. Reclaim the bride. Pierce the illusion.
You are Rāma.

www.ingramcontent.com/pod-product-compliance
Lightning Source LLC
Chambersburg PA
CBHW040524020526
44111CB00055B/2945